Here's what readers arc saying about The Traveling Tea Ladies!

"Melanie Salyers has done it again! Escaping inside the latest installment of The Traveling Tea Ladies (cup of tea at my side, of course!) was great fun, and by the end I was dying to know where Amelia and friends are headed in the third book!"

Melisa Wells
Author of *Chicken In The Car* and *The Car Won't Go*

"Talk about a perfect book to read at the beach ... entertaining and intriguing! Melanie O'Hara-Salyers is a young woman whose background of owning a tea room has provided the perfect experiences for her unique books about the traveling tea ladies!

The Traveling Tea Ladies Death in Dixie is a story that shows the deep friendships and loyalty of four friends who share an acute interest in tea. I found myself making notes of certain types of tea to try and could almost taste some of the tea foods and candy the author described.

This second book of Melanie's does make you wonder what can happen to these creative and resourceful women's next. I can't wait- the next book will take place in Savannah!"

Kathy Knight
ACCENT Editor, *The Greeneville Sun*

"I guarantee that once you start this book you will not be able to put it down. In fact I was so connected to the storyline that I almost missed my train stop. Rarely do I find a book that can capture my attention so deeply that I forget I am riding to work on the noisy NYC subway. I highly recommend this book. It's perfect for a book club or to give your best friend as a gift. Every time I sat down to read this book I felt I was getting together with my closest friends. It is a true gem indeed. I cannot wait to read about the next adventure the Traveling Tea Ladies take on."

Patty Aizaga
NYCGirlAtHeart.com

The Traveling Tea Ladies
DEATH IN DIXIE

Melanie O'Hara-Salyers

LYONS LEGACY PUBLISHING™

Johnson City, Tennessee

The Traveling Tea Ladies™
Death in Dixie

Cover art by Susi Galloway
www.SusiGalloway.com

Book design by Longfeather Book Design
www.longfeatherbookdesign.com

LYONS
LEGACY
PUBLISHING™

You may contact the publisher at:
Lyons Legacy Publishing™
123 East Unaka Aveneue
Johnson City, Tennessee 37601
Publisher@LyonsLegacyPublishing.com

ISBN: 978-0-9836145-0-0

For Olivia—The Brave Heart
I love you very much!

FOREWORD

I am so excited to have another Traveling Tea Ladies adventure in my hands! These ladies put me in the mind of *Steel Magnolias* sharing a cuppa with *Murder, She Wrote*. Feels like you're sitting down with some good friends to share "You'll never believe what happened on vacation!" stories, or perhaps wrapping yourself in a favorite throw to sit in your most comfy easy chair with a nice, hot cup of tea on the table next to you as you read a good old-fashioned letter from a treasured friend.

Author Melanie O'Hara-Salyers brings to bear her expertise as Miss Melanie of Miss Melanie's Tea Room & Gourmet Tea Emporium *and* owner of The Tea Academy as she relates the experiences of this tight-knit group of ladies whose lives intertwined thanks to The Pink Dogwood Tea Room. In the *Death In Dixie* adventure, Melanie deftly uses her storytelling craft to bring us to the National Storytelling Festival in nearby Jonesborough, Tennessee along with Amelia, Cassandra, Sarah, and Olivia as they rush to the aid of their friend Lucy, owner of Lyla's Tea Room. What starts out as cut-throat business practices that could put Lucy out of business during the National Storytelling Festival, quickly spirals downward into murder with all the signs pointing to Lucy as the culprit.

I can't help but applaud Sarah's time in the spotlight in this adventure, since I can so closely identify with the character of Sarah as a fellow Librarian turned tea lady. We're kindred spirits and I find it delightful that Sarah plays a pivotal role in solving this mystery as she applies her research skills to local ghost stories (shivers!) of Jonesborough! So hop on board this wild ride with The Traveling Tea Ladies: Death In Dixie—be careful not to spill your tea!

Kathryn Isaacs, Owner KTeas Specialty Tea & Gifts
Former Federal & State Publications Cataloger,
Library of Virginia
Blogger, "Of Life and Tea"

ACKNOWLEDGEMENTS

It has taken a village to bring this book to life. I would like to express my appreciation and gratitude to my tribe.

A special thank you to Jeannie Snyder for sharing her editing expertise and friendship.

Thank you to Jim O'Hara for story line editing and for always being a great Dad.

Thank you to Phyllis Estepp for making a difference in the lives of so many children and for your encouragement and guidance.

A standing ovation for artist Susi Galloway. You expertly took the ladies to the next level and created a gorgeous cover.

Thank you to Erik and Robert Jacobson for giving the ladies a voice through outstanding book design. You have been a true pleasure to work with.

To my real life Shane Spencer, my husband Keith, thank you for your constant encouragement, love and creative collaboration.

And thank you to my children, Olivia and Charlie. Remain close and stay strong no matter what life brings you and you will weather the storm. I am so proud to be your Mom!

The Traveling Tea Ladies
DEATH IN DIXIE

"*I* think the tea room looks great, Sarah!" I said as I put the finishing touches on the scarecrow for the front porch.

I had to admit—Sarah was doing a wonderful job decorating, organizing and running The Pink Dogwood Tea Room since I had sold it to her a year ago. Giving up "The Pink Lady" as I affectionately called this Victorian regal beauty had been a difficult decision for Shane and me, but I couldn't imagine anyone else doing a better job than Sarah. And, from what the guests were all telling me, she had enthusiastically infused her creative personality into new recipes for the savories and sweets on the tea tray. If her phone was any indication of how successful the transition had been, I'd say she was doing quite well. It had been ringing non-stop all morning!

"I really appreciate you coming over to help this morning, Amelia," Sarah said as she stepped back and smiled at the progress. "This is definitely a two woman job!" She fluffed the corn stalks that adorned the large white columns on the front porch and peeled back some of the dried husks to reveal whole ears of corn. She was dressed a bit like the *Farmer in the Dell* with her overalls and red and white checked long sleeved shirt. Her brunette hair was in braids secured with red ribbons. That was Sarah, dressed for the part.

"I think we need a few more bales of straw around the sign and we will be done," Sarah announced stepping back and admiring her handy work.

"I think Olivia mentioned she might be dropping off a few extra bales this afternoon," I told her. Olivia Rivers owned Riverbend Ranch, a therapeutic horseback riding center. Olivia along with our good friend, Cassandra Reynolds, rounded out our close knit group of four known as "The Traveling Tea Ladies." Recently, the four of us had returned from our latest tea traveling tour of Paris. Cassandra and I had spent a few weeks in "the city of lights," developing a line of tea-infused truffles for her company, Reynolds's Candies. Olivia, Sarah, and our respective significant others had joined us to spend the Christmas holidays and New Year's in Paris. It was a trip I will never forget! I was looking forward to a fruitful business partnership between Reynolds's Candies and my company, Smoky Mountain Coffee, Herb and Tea.

"I'll have to make sure I have plenty of peach iced tea ready and an extra large slice of blueberry almond sour cream pie to thank her," Sarah said laughing. Olivia was a hard worker, a good friend and was famous for her ravenous appetite and sassy attitude to match her auburn hair.

Sarah had really blossomed since she had become an entrepreneur. The quiet and meek Dogwood Cove librarian had transformed right before my eyes into a confident business woman. Oh, believe me! She still dressed in her themed outfits and "Sally Jesse Raphael" red oversized glasses, but instead of appearing outlandish and quirky as she had in the past, she now primarily dressed to complement the literary teas she was hosting at The Pink Dogwood Tea Room. It was amazing to see how she had infused her love of reading with her love of afternoon tea, offering such themed tea parties based on her favorite classics such as *Anne of Green Gables, Little Women* and *Gone With The Wind.* Her green velvet Scarlett O'Hara dress complete with hoop skirt and petticoat was by far my favorite of her literary costumes.

She had given up renting her small cottage on the edge of town when she purchased "The Pink Lady" and was now experiencing the joys of living in the historic downtown area, turning the second floor of the tea room into her personal quarters. She had added her own creative flare to the upstairs and loved the joys of being a homeowner for the first time.

"This is by far my favorite time of year," I told Sarah as I continued potting the colorful mums in shades of burnt orange, bright gold, and deep burgundy into the large urns on the front porch. "We are so lucky to have the wraparound views of the Smoky Mountains as far as the eye can see!"

Dogwood Cove was a jewel nestled in the shadows of the Great Smoky Mountains. Each year we hosted such events as The Dogwood Cove Apple Festival and we were famous across the U.S. for our beautiful spring season, when the Dogwood trees were in bloom in shades of light to dark pink and white. The year round mild temperatures and relatively small size of the town made Dogwood Cove very appealing for young families. We recently were named one of the top 20 towns in America by *Travel Magazine.*

"Why don't we take a tea break and reward ourselves for all this hard work," Sarah said and put her arm across my shoulders.

"I have a batch of sweet potato scones that I baked this morning which would be perfect with a pot of the new spiced Ceylon tea you brought over."

One of the many perks of owning The Smoky Mountain Coffee, Herb and Tea Company with my husband, Shane, was that I am surrounded by the intoxicating aromas of tea all day. I also got to experiment with blending new flavor combinations like the spiced Ceylon blend I had brought Sarah, but most importantly, I was able to make lifelong friends with each of my customers.

When I owned The Pink Dogwood Tea Room, Shane and I had also started our wholesale coffee and tea company in the hopes of making work easier on me. Not many people realize the long hours you put into owning your own business. Coupled with doing all the cooking and baking myself, I was often up at 3 o'clock in the morning making batches of scones by hand and creating tempting desserts for the tea tray. I had always considered baking to be therapeutic, but I had to admit, being able to sleep in until 6 o'clock was a much easier lifestyle for me and my family.

I brushed the dirt off my gloves and followed Sarah inside. Today I had my shoulder length dark blonde hair pulled back in a smooth pony tail and had worn my favorite gardening jeans and clogs. I removed the large straw brimmed hat that my dermatologist insisted I wear to protect my fair Irish skin.

"I love the harvest garland you have wrapped around the banister, Sarah! I never would have thought of using grapevine and berries in such a creative way," I told her as we walked into the front entry. The winding stair case was well over 100 years old and made such a dramatic entrance. Many brides through the years had posed on this staircase for their bridal portraits.

"Amelia, I'm so glad you like it! I have to admit how nervous I was when I bought the Pink Dogwood from you. I didn't know if I could do as good a job as you have in the past," Sarah said a bit sheepishly.

"Sarah, you have added so much of yourself and come up with so many clever ideas. I love the way you have embraced each of the seasons," I told her. "This place looks like a photo shoot for *Southern Living Magazine*."

Swags of fall leaves, pumpkins and berries were scattered across the eight mantles and antiques throughout the house. Sarah had cleverly decorated using a harvest theme and incorporated it right down to the last detail such as the collection of acorn and pumpkin shaped teapots displayed, oh so carefully, for sale in the gift shop. She was doing a marvelous job and needed no input from me.

"Why don't I start steeping the tea? You sit down and rest. You've put in a full morning's work," she insisted and patted a stool at the kitchen bar for me to sit down. It was good to be back in the familiar space in which I had spent so many hours working.

Sarah had the hot water ready and first filled the antique tea pot with water before quickly pouring it out to "preheat" the pot. She then measured the tea with a tea caddy, one teaspoon of tea for each cup of water, carefully spooning the tea into a paper filter designed to hold loose tea. She placed the filter into the teapot and refilled it with hot water. A quick four minutes on the tea timer and the tea would be ready.

She quickly moved about the kitchen, placing two beautiful sweet potato scones on Wedgewood autumn vine plates, adding small ramekins filled with homemade lemon curd and apple butter to accompany them. The aromas in the kitchen were heavenly.

"I've really missed being here," I told her, my eyes becoming teary. "This was my home away from home. Just being in this kitchen brings back so many memories." I smiled at Sarah as she patted my hand for comfort.

"Well, if you ever want to come back, just let me know!" she said with a gleam in her eye. We both started laughing and I quickly got over the lump in my throat.

"I think the "Pink Lady" is in good hands and let's leave it at that!" I said laughing. The tea timer went off and I inhaled the exotic aroma of cinnamon, cloves and orange peel as Sarah carefully filled each of our tea cups.

"Oh, Amelia!" she exclaimed. "This tea smells so delicious. I can't wait to try it."

"Oh, I'm glad you like it. I'm hoping it will be a best seller this fall and holiday season. I'm very proud of this blend." And I was. I enjoyed working side by side with Shane, creating new flavor combinations, increasing our advertising to include several national magazines devoted to tea lovers, and watching our client base grow. Yes, it had been a good decision and I truly had no regrets.

The phone rang and Sarah quickly answered it on the second ring. "Thank you for calling The Pink Dogwood Tea Room," she paused. "She's right here. Just one moment, please. It's for you," she said handing the phone to me.

"For me? Who would be calling me here?" I asked, taking the phone. "Hello, this is Amelia Spencer," I said into the receiver.

"Amelia! Thank goodness I found you! I hope you don't mind, but Shane told me you were at The Pink Dogwood today and I just have to talk with you!" a highly excited voice shouted on the phone.

"Lucy? Lucy? Is that you?" I asked caught off guard. "Are you okay?"

"Yes it's me and NO! NO! I'm not okay!" She said as her voice began to tremble. "She's trying to put me out of business!"

"What? Who is trying to put you out of business?" I asked even more confused. I covered the phone and whispered to Sarah, "It's Lucy Lyle from Lyla's Tea Room in Jonesborough. Something is terribly wrong with her." I listened intently to Lucy as she continued.

"Cheryl. That WITCH CHERYL is trying to put me out of business. She just bought the building directly across the street from me and is opening a tea bar. Can you imagine the nerve of her? And to top it off, she came over this morning and dropped off a flyer for their grand opening next week, just in time for the National Story Telling Festival!"

Lucy Lyle had owned and operated Lyla's Tea Room for the past ten years in Jonesborough, Tennessee's oldest town. Nestled in Northeast Tennessee, Jonesborough was just a short half hour drive from Dogwood Cove. Lucy and I were always quick to refer guests who might be traveling between the two towns to each other's tea rooms and we had partnered up in the past for special tea related events at the Women's Expo and

Bridal Shows. She ordered all of her tea from Smoky Mountain Coffee, Herb and Tea Company and being so close, I often personally delivered her tea orders and got caught up with the latest in Jonesborough. Plus, my Aunt Imogene lived in Jonesborough and it gave me an opportunity to meet her for a nice afternoon tea while I was there doing business.

"This is the first I've heard about a tea room opening in Jonesborough. Aunt Imogene keeps me pretty caught up with the gossip in town. I can't believe she didn't know about this. Are you sure?" I asked Lucy.

"Oh, I'm sure all right. I just heard it from the horse's mouth! The nerve of her!" Lucy was really fired up. I had never known her to be so upset before. But, I couldn't blame her. Jonesborough was a small tourist town with a single main street. Two tea rooms would be too much and Lyla's was an established icon in the area.

"Well, let's remain calm until we know all the facts. Who is this Cheryl woman anyway?" I asked her.

"Cheryl White is her name and she has caused a wake of trouble all over Jonesborough. I cannot stand this woman!" she told me snarling, the bitterness evident in her voice.

"Cheryl White. Cheryl White. That name sounds familiar," I said thoughtfully.

Sarah gasped and covered her mouth with her hand, "That's Jake's cousin, the one who moved back from Florida after her rich husband died." The color drained from her face as her mouth gaped open. "This is all my fault!"

"What?" I asked Sarah.

"Amelia. Amelia. Are you there?" Lucy shrieked loudly.

"Lucy. Let me call you right back. Better yet, I think I will head your way and talk with you some more about this." I tried my best to reassure her. "Everything will be okay."

"I hope you are right. Thanks Amelia and I will see you soon." The line went dead.

"Oh, no. Oh, no! This is entirely my fault!" Sarah said. "I should have known what she was up to when she started asking so many questions about the tea room."

"Wait. How do you know her?"

"She Jake's cousin by marriage. You remember me telling you about the funeral in Destin? Remember the big fight at the funeral home between Cheryl and her two step-daughters? It looked like a scene straight off the set of *The Real Housewives of New Jersey!*"

"Just vaguely, Sarah. What were they fighting about? I don't remember," I told her as I took another bite of sweet potato scone. The world might be falling apart, but I was not about to miss one crumb of these moist delicious morsels.

"Cheryl's husband owned a lot of beach front property in Destin. His daughters managed the properties for his company and they were under the impression that their father was leaving the business to them in his will. Instead, he left everything to Cheryl, his much younger wife," she informed me and began wiping down the counters nervously. "She came into town a few weeks ago to visit Jake and his parents and they brought her here for afternoon tea. This is my fault!" She threw down the cleaning cloth and covered her face with both of her hands, pushing her brown bangs straight up in the air.

Jake White was Sarah's "on-again, off-again" boyfriend

and was a reporter for *The Dogwood Daily*, our local newspaper. They had been dating for a couple of years and I hoped one day they might decide to make things official. They seemed like a good match, but only time would tell.

"Okay. Back up and begin at the beginning, Sarah," I said and walked over to her and gently removed her hands from her face. "How is it your fault?"

"Well, Cheryl was asking me all about owning a tea room. I was just so excited. I really didn't think anything of her questions, except at the time, I remember thinking she was a little pushy and nosey," she said calming down a bit.

"Pushy and nosey? How?" I inquired taking a seat again on the stool.

"Well, where did I order my tea? What was in my chicken salad? How much did I pay my servers? Where did my teapots come from? Things like that."

"Did you answer her?"

"Well, kind of," she said hesitating. "I didn't want to be rude in front of Jake and his family." Sarah began twirling her hair, a sure sign she was deep in thought.

"I think she is pushy. It's amazing what people will ask you and expect you to answer like what's the secret ingredient in your signature cream of tomato soup or can they have the recipe? If you share it, it won't be special anymore," I reminded her. "Don't let someone bully you into knowing all your trade information. You paid for this place and the recipes, not her." I was a firm believer in that.

"I think I've learned a very valuable lesson, just too late for Lucy, I'm afraid."

"Look, don't worry. I'm going to head over to Lucy's right now. I'll call Aunt Imogene and see what more I can find out. If anyone knows anything about Jonesborough, it's her!"

Aunt Imogene was a million dollar club realtor in Jonesborough and the surrounding Tri-cities area comprised of Johnson City, Kingsport and Bristol. She made it a priority to know the private business of everyone in town. I loved her, but she could be somewhat of a trouble maker, though not intentionally. She just didn't seem to have a filter from her brain to her mouth and most often spoke without thinking.

One incident with Aunt Imogene that comes to mind was at my engagement party when she stood up to make a toast and said, "Well, if you two get a few good years out of this marriage and he helps to raise the children, it will be worth it if you get divorced." That's Aunt Imogene for you! She really didn't mean to offend anyone, but it sort of happens anyway.

"Give my love to your Aunt. I just love the way she dresses!" Sarah said with a smile.

"Only you would appreciate her, Sarah." I hugged her and thanked her for the scones. "I'll call you when I find out something more. In the meantime, don't talk to Cheryl!" I warned.

"Tick-a-lock!" she said and gestured with her hand across her mouth as if she was zipping her lips closed and turning a key to lock them. It's an old Southern saying.

I jumped into "Ladybug," my red VW bug convertible with a black rag top and took off my gardening clogs. Thankfully I had a pair of comfortable Clark's in my trunk. I pulled out my cell phone while I sat in the driveway. I quickly dialed Shane at work to fill him in on where I was headed.

"Hello, Sweetie!" he said as he answered.

"What if it wasn't me?" I teased him.

"I have caller I.D!" He reminded me. "Where are you? I thought you would be back by now?"

"Well, I'm going to make a trip to Lyla's in Jonesborough and then head home."

"Okay. Are you meeting Aunt Imogene?" he asked with a hint of amusement in his voice.

"I might. I'll have to call her and see if she has time," I told him rolling the windows down to catch the cross breeze.

"You might be a while, then. You know how Imogene loves to gossip," he said teasingly.

"Gossip? Aunt Imogene? I don't know what you're talking about?" I said sarcastically.

"Well, if it gets too late, I'm sure Charlie and Emma won't mind if you stop at Pal's to bring home some "frenchie fries" and a Big Pal's burger!" Shane said with hope in his voice.

"You mean YOU won't mind if I stop at Pal's. Okay, I'll swing by one on the way home!" Pal's is a Tri-cities institution and was famous for its "Sudden Service" and inspirational quotes of the day like "Change Your Oil" or "Call Your Mom." The drive thru chain started in 1956 and was also famous for its gigantic hotdogs, hamburgers and fries on top of its aqua blue free-standing buildings.

I quickly told him goodbye and turned off my phone. I started the engine, eased "Ladybug" out of the driveway and onto I-26 for the 30 minute drive to Jonesborough.

TWO

I found a space in front of Lyla's Tea Room and smoothly eased "Lady Bug" into a parallel parking spot. Jonesborough was adorned with corn stalk bundles wrapped around every antique lamp post, bales of hay topped with pumpkins by every store front door, and National Story Telling flags flying from the lamp posts. The town had a welcoming feel to it and a homespun comfortable look. National Story Telling Festival was held annually the first weekend in October.

"Oh, Amelia, I'm so glad you are here!" Lucy cried and gave me a quick bear hug. She pulled me through the front entrance to the tea room "I feel like such a ninny calling you, but I didn't know who else to talk to," she whimpered.

Lucy was in her mid 50's with graying hair that she kept cut in a chin length "wash and go" hair cut. She seemed to not pay much attention to her wardrobe—she was far too practical to care. She was more concerned with wearing comfortable shoes and basic solid slacks and shirts under her tea room apron rather than be a slave to fashion.

"I'm glad you did call me," I told her following her into the quaint and cozy tea room. The bead board paneled walls painted a soft antique white gave the feeling that one had stepped back in time. Small intimate tables for two were positioned by the original antique windows to take advantage of the natural light. Scattered tables for four were covered in burgundy tablecloths and topped with lace overlays. The setting and effect made Lyla's the perfect spot for ladies who lunched and those that indulged in a traditional afternoon tea.

"I called Aunt Imogene to meet us. Maybe she can shed some light on this Cheryl White."

"You mean Cheryl WITCH!" Lucy spat out. Several of her guests who had been engaged in low conversations, turned and looked in her direction.

"Let's sit down somewhere a bit more private," I said and took Lucy by the elbow. I guided her away from the awkward stares of some of her patrons.

"We really don't want any of your guests seeing you this angry," I suggested.

I walked Lucy towards a more private table tucked back in the corner of Lyla's Tea Room. She sat down, limp like a rag doll as if all of the life had been knocked right out of her.

"Well, more than a few people got an earful earlier today when she sashayed in here with her flyers. I can't believe she came into MY TEA ROOM and put those down on MY COUNTER and asked if I would pass these out to my guests! It just goes to show you that just because you have money, doesn't mean you have an ounce of class!" Lucy was pounding both her fists on the table for emphasis. More than one patron looked nervously around at us. I steadied our tea cups on their saucers that were jumping around each time Lucy made contact with the table.

"Lucy, get a grip before you drive your business away!" I told her placing my hands on top of her fists, trying to keep her from hitting the table again. "You are acting like a crazy person!"

"I feel like I'm crazy!" she admitted, in a whisper. "I didn't work to build this tea room from the ground up to watch some sort of 'Cruella DeVille' come in here and tear it all down."

" 'Cruella DeVille?' " I asked surprised. "Isn't that description a bit much?"

"You haven't met her, Amelia! She's systematically buying up property in Jonesborough. And to top it off, she's been taking a lot of business away from the shop keepers in our area. She's trouble, Amelia! Real trouble for all of us!"

"Woo Hoo, Amelia, honey!" Aunt Imogene called loudly and began waving as she came through the front door to Lyla's. She made a direct bee-line to our table, decked out in a one piece leopard jumpsuit and matching chandalier leopard earrings, the size of tea cup saucers. Her short brunette hair was teased and poofed high. Her four inch stilettos in matching animal print click-clacked across the floor as her ample bottom swayed back and forth. She looked like she was a groupie for Sigfried and Roy.

"Hi, Aunt Imogene!" I said as I rose from my chair. She gave me an "air" kiss on both cheeks before she put her over-sized zebra handbag down with a thump on the floor and took a seat.

"What are you two girls up to today?" she asked as she took out her compact to check her bright lipstick, the shade of the day "fire engine red." She carefully began applying another coat and smacked her lips together to evenly spread the lipstick.

"Well, Aunt Imogene. We were just talking about a new property owner in Jonesborough and wondered if you might know her. Cheryl White?" I said as I lowered my voice to a discreet level.

"Oh, the gold digger from Destin?" she said non-chalantly. "Yeah, I know her. Why do you ask?" She put away her compact and lipstick and looked directly at me. That was Aunt Imogene, blunt and to the point.

"Well, she purchased the building directly across the street and plans on opening a tea bar. She told Lucy she's going to put her out of business," I informed her.

Imogene quickly turned her head in Lucy's direction. "Hmm. Well, I heard something about that, but I was hoping it wasn't true. You know how gossipy people are in Jonesborough." She took out a toothpick and began picking at her teeth. "Really, if people would just mind their own business, the shop keepers would get along so much better," she concluded.

Was this the pot calling the kettle black or what? I thought to myself.

"What do you know about her, Aunt Imogene?" I leaned closer, hoping it would encourage her to keep her voice down. Too late! It didn't deter her.

"Well!" she announced looking around Lyla's hoping to grab everyone's attention, "I do know that her husband left her well-off as in thirty million dollars well off, and she's spending it like money grows on trees. Why she was just in at Massengail's in downtown Johnson City and spent three thousand dollars this morning on an evening gown for the 'Dogwood and Cattails Ball.' Can you believe that?"

The Dogwood and Cattails Ball was an annual event to raise money for the Washington County, Tennessee Humane Society. Four legged guests often showed up with their owners for the charity evening. I had considered taking Lily, the tea room porch kitty, but decided she might not enjoy rubbing fur with some of the larger dogs that regularly attended.

"How do you know that?" I asked Imogene.

"Honey, because I was having my hair cut and colored at Salon Nouveaux and over heard Marge telling Beverly about it at the next station. But, you didn't hear that from me!" she said and winked. This was sounding more and more like a scene from *Steel Magnolia's* and "Trudy's Beauty Shop." All that was missing was Dolly Parton, one of our state's greatest treasures.

"Okay. I'll keep it our little secret!" I winked back. If Imogene knew, everyone would know by sundown.

"That doesn't count the doggy outfit she purchased from 'Paws and Claws.' That set her back another couple hundred for the feathered boa and sequined blue ensemble." She informed us and pushed back from the table. "But you didn't hear that from me."

"Aunt Imogene, you are just a wealth of information. How do you do it?" I teased her.

"I'm a realtor. It's my job to know who is divorcing, who got fired, who's moving," she said rather proudly. She leaned back in her chair and puffed her chest out.

"Let's focus on this tea bar she has planned across the street," Lucy said in a frustrated tone. "What do you know about that?"

"I heard she's snatching up real estate all over Jonesborough as if she's playing Monopoly. She's trying to tie all her assets up because her step-daughters are livid about their father's will and are protesting it in court next month. She bought the old Salt House building as well as the Parson's Table. She's planning on opening a dinner theatre and gift shops. You aren't the only shop owner who is worried. Anyone else hungry?"

Lucy took her cue from Imogene and headed towards the kitchen. She first circulated around the dining room to check on her guests and grabbed pitchers of iced tea to refill glasses.

The Salt House, built in 1864, was a distribution warehouse for salt during the Civil War. Since then it has been used as an office building, Masonic Hall and a grocery store. More recently, it had been an upscale gift shop.

Construction of the Parson's Table was halted in 1870 due to the cholera epidemic. Though it currently was used as a restaurant, in its former life it served as a church and a temporary storehouse for coffins during the epidemic.

Lucy came out of the kitchen and presented our table with a tray laden with three steaming bowls of pumpkin bisque and a large pot of tea. She sat down, her hands visibly trembling.

"Thank you, Lucy," I said taking her hand. "It's going to be all right. You've got ten years of stable business experience and reputation on her."

"Absolutely," Imogene agreed and took a long drawn out slurp of her soup. "Everyone who's anyone takes afternoon tea at Lyla's," she said matter-of-factly. She returned to busily eating the bisque.

"But Cheryl's tea bar is going to be like a Starbucks, more like a "Teabucks" with wi-fii, chrome fixtures—very modern," Lucy whined. She picked up the teapot and attempted to pour each of us a cup, but her nerves got the best of her and she knocked a tea cup over in the process.

"Here, Lucy. Allow me to pour," I told her as I inhaled the heady scent of the tea. "Is this Russian Caravan? It smells so delightful!" Russian Caravan is a blend of Formosa oolong and a hint of lapsang souchong creating a strong cup of tea with smoky undertones.

"Lucy, there are as many different types of tea rooms as there are different personality types of tea room owners," I soothed her. "You have the ambiance of historic Jonesborough. I really don't see how a tea bar will go over on Main Street in these refurbished buildings. Plus, we are several miles from the nearest downtown office area and East Tennessee State University is more than eight miles away. The kids aren't going to drive here to go to a tea bar," I reasoned. "She would be better off being in a location closer to the college or downtown Johnson City," I concluded, convincing myself as much as Lucy.

"You're right, Amelia. I don't know why I got so upset," Lucy shook her head, soothing herself. "I just got scared that a little competition would shake up my business and I've just worked too hard." She removed her glasses and rubbed her forehead, visibly stressed. She smoothed her apron repeatedly with both hands and gazed around her tea room. Lucy had worked her fingers to the bone to build up Lyla's and I knew the thought of losing her business had to be eating away at the pit of her whole being.

"Lucy, I will give you the same advice Shane gave me in a similar situation. Maintain! Maintain! Maintain! If you need to tweak a few recipes, now is the time to do it. Don't slash your prices and get into a price war. Just continue to do what you do best! Offer the best quality afternoon tea in Jonesborough and give perks for your loyal customers to keep them coming back!"

"You're right, Amelia. You're absolutely right." Lucy placed her glasses squarely back on her nose, a determined look fixed on her face.

"At first, everyone will want to check out her place, but then they'll be right back over here, happily eating at Lyla's again," Imogene said placing her spoon on her plate. "That was just wonderful! You'll have to share your recipe with me."

"No can do, Aunt Imogene," I chastised her. "Lucy's recipes are the difference between her business success and the success of the new tea bar. She should guard these recipes with her life."

"Well excuse em'moi Miss Amelia!" Imogene snipped. "I didn't realize that we were talking about the trademark for KFC's eleven secret spices." She opened her tote bag again and took out her compact and began surveying her face again.

"It wouldn't hurt me to be a bit more careful about my recipes and maybe do some new specials to keep repeat customers happy. Amelia, you have some wonderful ideas," Lucy said.

"I've been through a similar situation where someone decided to start a catering business from home and advertise themselves as the premier tea party caterer in Dogwood Cove. At first, it really shook me up, but I found out that she was operating illegally from her home without a health inspected kitchen and it soon caught up with her. It did help me to appreciate my business and to protect my recipes as well as my guest information."

"Oh, and Amelia had that hateful server who was copying e-mail addresses from her guest book and contacting them to promote her own side business," Imogene informed Lucy.

"Yes. I had almost forgotten about that. Business can be quite cut-throat, especially in a small town," I said, nodding my head in agreement.

My handbag began vibrating and I excused myself to take the phone call outside to keep from intruding on the other guests enjoying afternoon tea. If there was one thing I was a stickler about at The Pink Dogwood Tea Room, it was that cell phone calls be taken outside so as not to disturb the other guests' tea experiences.

"Hello?"

"Amelia, Liv here."

"Hey, Olivia!"

"Sarah and I were just enjoying some blueberry almond sour cream pie and that made me think of dinner."

"Only you, Liv, would think of dinner while you are eating dessert!" I teased her.

"Hey—I plan ahead. What can I say?" she laughed. "I'm firing the grill up and thought if you don't have any plans, we should get together for some BBQ tonight! I've already called Cassandra and she's coming. She's bringing the cocktails."

"That sounds like fun! I don't think Shane will mind since he asked me to pick up Pal's on the way home, so I'll give him a call and let him know that we're having a girl's night BBQ." Nothing beats dinner by the Tennessee River at Olivia's ranch. I was looking forward to some of her signature BBQ ribs and baked beans.

"Did you say you are going by Pal's?" She asked sounding very interested. "Any chance you could bring me a large 'frenchie fry' and a chocolate shake?" Pal's called their seasoned fries, "frenchie fries" and their peach tea, "peachie tea."

"You crack me up, Olivia! Only you would ask me to bring Pal's to a BBQ." I shook my head in amazement at how much Olivia was able to eat, yet maintain her petite frame. But, she did more manual work than the average man around Riverbend Ranch with baling hay, working the horses, and bush hogging the fields. She could repair barbed wire fencing, fix a leaking roof, and help birth a horse. She was amazing!

"Hey, look! I could have asked for a double Big Pal's. I controlled myself. I don't want to ruin dinner. I wish Dogwood Cove would have a Pal's franchise!"

"What time tonight, Liv?" I hoped I had time to go home and shower, change my clothes and whip up something yummy to bring.

"Seven sound good?"

"Seven sounds great. I will drop your Pal's off as soon as I get into Dogwood Cove so you can enjoy those fries while they are hopefully still hot!" I said.

"Thanks, Amelia. I'm getting hungry just thinking about it! See you soon!"

"Bye, Liv!"

I quickly ended the call and headed back inside Lyla's. Imogene was making the rounds, visiting with several of the ladies at the other tables. I caught Lucy's eye behind the twelve foot long antique bar that served as a tea preparation area as well as a display area for her delicious homemade cakes, pies and scones featured on dome covered cake stands. I watched her as she expertly sliced a hearty helping of mincemeat pie and placed the dome back over the pie. She topped the pie with a dollop of fresh whipped cream, dusted it with a pinch of cinnamon and placed it on the counter.

"Thank you again, Amelia, for coming. I appreciate you dropping everything to drive over today." She pushed her hair back behind her ears and once again, smoothed her apron with her hands, visibly still distressed.

"You and I go way back, Lucy! Of course I want to help. You have been a big part in helping to build Smoky Mountain Coffee, Herb and Tea Company. Shane and I owe you one!" I said patting her arm and giving it a reassuring rub.

"The downtown Jonesborough merchants will be having a meeting tomorrow night. If I find anything else out, I will give you a call." She pulled a tissue out of her apron pocket and began dabbing her eyes. "What am I going to do, Amelia?" She looked as though she was working herself into a full blown crying spell.

"Don't get upset prematurely. Stay calm. Get your facts together first. And you have friends in this community to count on!" I quietly told her.

"What's going on over here, Lucy?" Imogene asked joining us at the bar area.

"She's just upset about Cheryl. But, I told Lucy, she's going to be more than fine—she's going to be GREAT!"

"Honey, I for one will make sure all the Tri-cities realtors keep you in business. In fact, can I go ahead and schedule our next office meeting here? Would you be available next Monday at ten o'clock? Maybe we could do a breakfast brunch so we do not take up your tables during the lunch crowd?" Imogene asked getting out her datebook.

"How does artichoke quiche, fresh fruit salad and cherry scones sound for the menu?" Lucy asked with a slightly stuffy sounding nose. She began writing notes in her calendar to confirm the menu selection.

"Sounds amazing as always!" Imogene exclaimed giving air kisses to both of us. "Amelia, dear! I hope to see you and that good looking husband of yours soon."

"Bye Imogene. Bye Lucy. I'll be back this way for deliveries later this week. Keep me posted—ok?"

I hopped into "Lady Bug" and carefully maneuvered my way onto Main Street. For such a little town, they sure did have a lot of traffic and tourists. I hoped everything would work out for Lucy. Little did I know what tomorrow night's meeting would hold and who held all the cards!

THREE

Olivia did have the grill fired up and going when I pulled into the circular driveway of Riverbend Ranch. I could smell the ribs and BBQ sauce wafting from the plume of smoke coming from her back deck. The "Traveling Tea Ladies" had shared many wonderful meals over the years at this picturesque location that overlooked the Tennessee River.

"Amelia, sweetie! You look wonderful," Cassandra said as she hurried towards me with her arms open wide for a big hug. "Here, let me grab this basket before you drop it!"

"You look very chic tonight, Cassandra!" And she did with her aubergene turtleneck, matching poncho and purple suede boots, a perfect back drop to offset her five plus carat amethyst broach adorned with diamonds. A gift from Doug, no doubt, as he always enjoyed selecting the perfect piece of jewelry for Cassandra. He knew how to spoil her!

"Yes, I was telling Cassandra she looks just like a gigantic eggplant," Olivia called out from behind the large grill as smoke billowed in her face causing her to cough slightly.

"Well, at least I don't look like the calendar girl for Tractor Supply!" Cassandra replied with a big grin on her face. "That was a good one, I have to admit! Come on over here and fill us in on what's going on with Lucy. Sarah was just telling us something about Cheryl White." We walked over to the large knotty pine trestle table on the stone patio and I began unpacking my contribution of baked acorn squash with brown sugar and raisins as I retold the day's events in Jonesborough.

"Poor Lucy," Sarah said as she helped set the table with Olivia's Ralph Lauren equestrian china pattern that Cassandra had begun collecting for her. Olivia had been reluctant to own nice place settings, but when Cassandra showed her the bridles and buckles that adorned the border of the dinner plates, Olivia had conceded. Though the two swapped barbed comments from time to time, they were the closest of friends.

"I can't believe Cheryl would even think of opening a tea business right across the street from Lyla's. What is wrong with her?" Sarah said with total amazement in her voice. "I'm afraid this will cause a problem between Jake and me because apparently she has his parents fooled into thinking that she has been an absolute angel her entire life. They have no idea what she's like."

"Eventually, they will figure it out," Olivia reassured Sarah. "It's probably best if you don't say too much. Let them hear it through the grapevine." Olivia loaded a platter with ribs hot off the grill and placed them in the center of the table. "I'm hungry girls. Let's eat!" she exclaimed and began piling ribs, corn on the cob, acorn squash and homemade yeast rolls on her plate.

"Slow down, Liv. This isn't the KentuckyDerby!" Cassandra joked with her.

"Do you have any idea how long it's been since I've eaten today?" Olivia snapped back at her.

"Oh, probably a half an hour at the most, I'm guessing!"

Cassandra laughed and began buttering her steaming hot yeast roll. "Did you make these, Sarah? They look delicious!"

"Yes I did!" Sarah replied delighted with the praise. "I really have embraced baking since I bought the tea room."

"And everyone is embracing your new menu! Sarah is really infusing her personality into everything," I told the girls. "Cassandra is right! These yeast rolls are scrumptious!"

"You've got to put some of the cinnamon honey butter on them," Olivia informed us. She took a big bite of corn and continued. "Then they're perfect."

"How would you know?" Cassandra said carefully eyeing her.

"Because I had a few when Sarah first got here," Olivia told her.

"I thought you said you hadn't eaten for a while!" Cassandra had her on the ropes!

"I know. I know. Look, you don't understand my high metabolism. If I didn't eat several times a day, I would be emaciated!" She said defensively grabbing a rib.

"More like cranky!" Cassandra said and playfully swatted her arm.

"You're just jealous!" Olivia informed her. She smiled slyly at Cassandra and wiped BBQ sauce from the corner of her mouth with her napkin. She quickly took another bite of her ribs.

"We're all jealous of how much you can eat and not gain any weight!" I added. "What does Lincoln think of your appetite?" I asked her. Lincoln was Matt Lincoln, Olivia's steady boyfriend that she met while we were attending my class reunion at Southern Methodist University in Dallas, Texas. Matt had been instrumental in solving the murder of my college roommate, Emmy award winning actress, Katherine Gold.

"Lincoln loves me just the way I am," she said with one eyebrow raised as if she was challenging me.

"Did you say LOVE?" Cassandra squealed. "LOVES you the way you are?" Her mouth was open wide and she was excited.

"Before you start registering me for any more china patterns, I'm not sure how I feel about him."

"Olivia, it's not every day you meet someone as nice as Detective Lincoln," Sarah said with conviction. "I think you two are really lucky to have found each other." Sarah dabbed at the corner of her eyes with her napkin and smiled at Olivia, genuinely happy.

"Well, I don't know what to think," Olivia said and pushed her plate away. She picked up her napkin from her lap and began twisting it. "He wants to get married."

"Ah ha! I knew it!" Cassandra shrieked and began repeatedly pounding her five inch heels on the ground in rapid fire succession. "I knew he was the one for you from the first moment you laid eyes on him in the police station."

Olivia folded her arms and placed her head on the table. She definitely didn't seem like someone who was excited about the prospect of marriage at the moment.

"What's wrong, Liv?" I asked her and patted her arm. "Why don't you seem happy?"

"Olivia, don't screw this up!" Cassandra warned her. "If you let this man get away, I will personally hunt you down and shoot you myself!" She wagged her finger at Olivia.

"Look, Cassandra. You don't know how hard this is for me!" Olivia turned to face her. "This is really a very difficult decision for me to make."

"Difficult how? Cassandra asked. You have a gorgeous man who adores you, who loves you and you are having a hard time with that?"

"Look, before you begin selecting the bridesmaids dresses, there is something y'all need to know," she warned us.

"What is it? Just tell us!" I implored. "What's the big deal?"

"He wants me to move to DALLAS, that's what's the big deal is!" Olivia shouted.

We all were very quiet as we took in what she had shared with us. Olivia, move to Dallas? I didn't even want to think about what that would mean for our close-knit friendship and for the many families who had children enrolled in her therapeutic horseback riding center. Olivia was a vital part of our community and Riverbend Ranch had helped many handicapable children develop their fine motor skills. The ranch was just one of a handful in the country that used horses to develop emotional, cognitive and physical abilities for kids with special needs. Currently she had fifty children enrolled with a waiting list of one hundred more. Dogwood Cove needed Riverbend Ranch!

"Oh, honey. I didn't know," Cassandra said putting her arm around Olivia's shoulder. "Why didn't you say something?"

"Because I love him. But my life is here. He just doesn't understand. His whole world revolves around his career with the Dallas Metropolitan Police Department, and my life is more than one thousand miles away here at this ranch. He's asking me to give all this up for him." She shook her head and looked up to the sky. "I just can't make that kind of decision."

"Here, Liv. Have a sip of my 'Tea-tini,' " Cassandra said and slid a glass towards her. "You know, you don't have to make you mind up right now." She looked at Sarah and me and raised her eyebrows as if silently pleading for us to help."

"When did all this come up?" I asked Olivia, hoping I wasn't being too nosey.

"This past weekend when Lincoln flew out here for a visit. He proposed while we were hiking to Abrams Falls. It was beautiful. It was perfect, up until we began arguing about why his job was more important than mine."

Part of what made Matt Lincoln and Olivia Rivers such a good pair was that they were both driven in their work ethic and also both very devoted to their careers. Lincoln was a highly decorated Police Detective and was moving quickly up the ranks in the department. His tall, dark, good looks were quite a contrast to Olivia's petite height of five feet zero inches tall and her long wavy auburn hair. They did make such a stunning couple.

"Surely Lincoln understands how vital Riverbend Ranch is to the Dogwood Cove community?" I asked her.

"I can't believe he would ask me to give this all up, as if I could just pick up and start another program in Dallas. He doesn't understand how hard I have worked and sacrificed to build this."

And she had. It had taken Olivia years to get the federal grants to start the non-profit program, of which there were just a few in the Southeast. The closest therapeutic horseback riding center was Small Miracles in Kingsport, Tennessee, just twenty minutes outside of Jonesborough. They too had a waiting list of kids wanting to horseback ride.

"Maybe you should talk with him more about this and get him to understand," Cassandra suggested.

"No. I think we're through! Just when everything was going along so great," Olivia sighed and took a sip of the "Tea-tini". "Did you make this yourself, Cassandra? It's quite good."

"No, I had a little help with the 'Tea-tini'" Cassandra admitted. She was a self-proclaimed kitchen screw-up and had very little time to learn to cook. After all, she had Reynolds's Candies to run and her rolodex was filled with private caterers, ready to throw a dinner party together in short notice. Cassandra and her husband Doug enjoyed entertaining in simple, yet sophisticated style from their lake front home.

"Okay—let's table the talk about Lincoln and enjoy the barbeque," Olivia said taking a fork full of acorn squash. "Amelia, did you bring dessert tonight?" She asked hopefully.

"Cassandra and I have that covered with some of our tea infused chocolates. Would you like an Earl Grey or an orange blossom oolong truffle?" I smiled and took the box out of my basket. "I think we could all use a little chocolate therapy, don't you?"

"You know, dark chocolate is full of antioxidants, it is also good for your heart and releases endorphins into the body," Sarah said excited! "Plus, you are also receiving the antioxidants and polyphenols from the tea. It's like eating a cup of tea!"

"You sound like a walking advertisement for Reynolds's Candies," Olivia joked with her. "I don't' care what they are full of, I just want to devour them!" It was good to see she was shaking things off and her appetite had returned, at least for the moment. I knew she was really hurting on the inside and just putting up a good front for all of us.

We toasted to "The Traveling Tea Ladies" and clinked our glasses, enjoying the cool fall evening and the melody of the rushing water nearby. But, our thoughts were soon interrupted by my cell phone.

"Sorry, girls, it's Lucy! I better answer this," I told them.

"Hey, Lucy! I didn't expect to hear from you so soon."

"Amelia. I'm ruined. He's left and gone to work for her," she said dejectedly.

"Who's left?" I asked, confused.

"Chef Paul. He turned in his apron today and told me he's gone to work for Cheryl. And to top it all off, most of my wait staff is going with him, effective immediately!" She was barely keeping it together, the panic apparent in her voice.

"Are you sure he's going to work for Cheryl?" I couldn't believe this!

"He told me so himself. When I offered him a raise, he informed me Cheryl was paying him double his salary at Lyla's. I just can't compete with that. The National Story Telling Festival is just four days away and I have no chef and no wait staff. It's my busiest time of year. What am I going to do?" She started crying and my heart went out to her.

"When did you say your next Jonesborough merchant meeting was?" I asked with sudden inspiration.

"Tomorrow night," she sniffed into the phone.

"I'll be there with you. I want to meet this Cheryl White. In the meantime, can you handle cooking for the lunch crowd tomorrow by yourself?"

"Sure. I'll keep it simple. And my niece can help with serving. It will be like old times when I did all the cooking and baking myself."

"I'll give Imogene a call and see if we can't put our heads together and come up with a strategy," I was thinking aloud. "Will Cheryl be at the merchant's meeting?"

"Oh, yes. Most definitely. She is getting final approval to open, so the historical board will have to vote on quite a few things," she said.

"Things may not work out so smoothly for her. Let's remember the hiccups the historical board threw your way when you were trying to open," I reminded her.

"Yeah. Like approving paint color for the interior walls. I thought I was going to have to have an arm wrestling match with them over that. Who heard of only five colors being appropriate?" Lucy recalled.

"What time is the meeting tomorrow?"

"Six thirty at the court house."

"How 'bout I meet you at Lyla's around five o'clock tomorrow afternoon and we can put our heads together and do some brainstorming before the meeting," I suggested.

"Thank you, Amelia. I knew I could count on you."

"See you then, and Lucy….. try not to worry."

"I'll do my best. Bye, Amelia." We hung up and I turned to see three pairs of eyes staring at me in disbelief.

"What in the world?" Cassandra asked. "What's going on now with Lucy?"

"Chef Paul is now working for Cheryl White." I informed her.

"He's gone to 'The Dark Side,' " Olivia stated, crossing her arms and nodding her head in the affirmative.

"Yep. He traded in a good job with an honest employer and took most of the wait staff with him," I stated.

"He sold his soul is what he did," Sarah said with a stern look on her face.

"How many years has he worked for Lucy?" Cassandra asked, in total disbelief. "Hasn't it been about eight years?"

"Something like that. I remember they won 'Taste of Jonesborough' together with her pumpkin bisque. She was even written up in *Tea Time Magazine* for that recipe. Chef Paul and Lucy have developed some wonderful menus over the years," I said in a daze. "Why would he want to go and throw away a perfectly great work relationship for the unknown?"

"Sounds like greed," Olivia stated leaning back and set her boots up on the corner of the table in an authoritative pose. "She's promised him something, I'd wager."

"You're right. Double his salary," I agreed.

"Wow. Can Lucy afford to meet that?" Sarah asked incredulously.

"No. She can't. But she can't afford to lose him either," I speculated.

"What is she going to do?" Sarah asked with worry in her voice.

"Well, she's going to have to get a new chef and pronto," Olivia said in a flat tone, deep in thought.

"And an entirely new wait staff," Sarah added.

"Oh, gosh! I just realized, if Chef Paul left, he can replicate all of Lucy's signature menu items!" I exclaimed.

"She needs to start over with a new menu or hope Cheryl isn't interested in her recipes," Cassandra suggested. Now we were all worrying for Lucy.

"Oh, I imagine part of why Cheryl is paying Chef Paul such a high salary is because she is after the recipes. If he didn't sign a non-compete contract with Lucy, he can take ALL the recipes with him," I told them.

"Oh, dear! This is not sounding good at all. I just feel sick about all of this," Sarah quietly murmured. "If I hadn't been so enthusiastic about The Pink Dogwood Tea Room, she never would have come up with the idea of opening a tea business."

"Sarah, people do what they really want to do," Olivia said succinctly. "Cheryl wanted to have a fight with someone. What she wasn't counting on was us!"

"Us?" Cassandra asked surprised.

"Yeah, us! Come on, Cassandra! You have an army of award winning chefs over at Reynolds's. Can't you loan Lucy someone temporarily until she can find time to hire a permanent replacement?" Olivia urged. She quickly turned to face the rest of us and continued. "And Sarah, you've told me that you have connections with some of the sorority girls at East Tennessee State. Maybe they could give Lucy a hand by waiting tables and doing some dishes. I'm sure they could use the extra paychecks right before fall break!"

"Olivia—you are a genius!" I told her. "Why didn't I think of that?" I jumped up from the table and ran over to the opposite side to give her a big hug from behind.

"Amelia, please. Don't over react!" she cried pushing me off.

"Oh, get over yourself, Olivia and accept the thanks! Just

for that, another hug," I said squeezing her harder.

"Ok—so Sarah will talk with the sorority girls at ETSU, Cassandra will lend a little culinary expertise from Reynolds's, and I will attend the meeting with Lucy tomorrow to meet this Cheryl White and see what's going on." It was a plan and one that I thought would be quite effective.

"I'm going to Jonesborough with you, Amelia." Olivia quickly said.

"Me too!" Cassandra added.

"Count me in!" Sarah piped up.

"What for?" I asked surprised.

"If there's one thing I can't stand, it's someone with a little bit of money pushing good people like Lucy around," said Olivia. "I need to go out to Small Miracles anyway and talk with their therapy director. Jonesborough is on the way." She popped a chocolate truffle in her mouth. "Mmm, whoa! I really can taste the orange blossom oolong in that candy. I love that, Amelia! Those are excellent."

"And I personally feel responsible for Cheryl even getting the idea of owning a tea business, so I would like to help Lucy in any way I can," Sarah added uneasily. "I will ask Bonnie if she can run things for a day or two in my absence." Bonnie had been Sarah's right hand since she had bought The Pink Dogwood Tea Room. Bonnie was an excellent manager and would relish the opportunity to take the reins in Sarah's absence.

"Why don't we make a weekend out of it?" Cassandra suggested. "I'll call the Carnegie Hotel in Johnson City and see if we can still get a room so close to the National Story Telling Festival weekend. We could also book a visit to the Austin

Springs Spa at the hotel. Huh? How does that sound?" She was getting excited.

"I say you're on!" I told her enthusiastically!

"All right then. It's settled!" Cassandra giggled. "Another adventure for 'The Traveling Tea Ladies!'" We refilled the "Tea-tinis" and watched the sun setting.

Sometimes when you think you have everything tied up with a neat little bow, you can find the best laid plans quickly unraveling, right before your very eyes!

FOUR

"*I* think it's great you are helping Miss Lucy, Mom!" Emma said over a breakfast of Irish oatmeal with dried cranberries.

"Are you going to be staying at Aunt Imogene's?" she asked as she finished her orange juice and started hoisting her bulging backpack over her shoulder.

"Not this time, sweetie. We are staying at the Carnegie Hotel in Johnson City," I told her and helped to lift the giant backpack. *How did these kids get through the day with such a heavy load?* I wondered.

"The hotel across from the mini-dome?" Charlie asked excitedly. He was growing up so fast, but still had his boyish freckles that I loved so much. Where did the time go?

"Yes, across from the mini-dome. But, there are no basketball games this time of year, so I don't think I'll be on campus for any reason."

"What if I asked you to get me an ETSU Buccaneers sweatshirt? Could I bribe you to go to the bookstore to get one? I'll mow the grass and take out the garbage for a month without allowance! Please Mom!" he begged.

"Gosh. I had no idea you wanted a sweat shirt so badly. I'd say you've got a deal!" I told him and smoothed his hair to the side. "Give me a quick kiss before you head off to school."

"Love you Mom," Charlie said and gave me a sweet peck on the cheek.

"Love you Mom. Be careful!" Emma reminded me sounding more like my mother than my teenage daughter.

"I love you both. I'll call y'all tonight after the meeting. Do your homework before any TV, okay?" I scolded them both with a smile on my face. "Have your Dad check your math, got it?"

"Got it, Mom!" they said in chorus and headed to the bus stop. It was a bit chilly this morning and I pulled my black wool wrap a bit tighter to ward off the cold.

"Got time for a pot of Irish Breakfast tea?" Shane asked, bringing me a steaming cup full.

"Oh, thank you! And thank you for encouraging me to help Lucy out."

"Lucy is one of our best customers and a great friend. I want her to ride this out and have much continued success with her tea room. She's a real peach," he said taking a seat on the porch and warming up with a cup of his favorite Guatemalan coffee. That was the great thing about the business. He loved his coffee. I loved my tea. We complemented each other very well.

"Are you sure this is not going to be too much on you right now? I sprung this on you with rather short notice." I took another slow sip of tea and felt my eyes opening up.

"I can handle the kids and work too. I've got a pretty good crew in place at Smoky Mountain. We just filled most of our large pre-holiday corporate orders, so I want you to go and not worry about what's going on here. We'll miss you, but we'll be okay. Besides, I've been promising the kids I would take them to a paint ball game and this weekend will be a good opportunity." He smiled and watched my face fill with worry.

"Paintball? Are you sure, Shane? Do you have all the protective eye wear, chest guards, all the body armor?"

"Amelia, it's not that bad. The kids will be fine," he reassured me. "I knew you would worry too much. That's why we're going while you are not here," he teased.

"You're the one I'm worried about, Shane Spencer," I said as I rose from my chair and sat down in his lap. "Remember the time I left for the 'Tea Cruise' and you decided to play football with your old college buddies? Need I say more?" I reminded him.

"A torn hamstring muscle is not going to happen during an innocent game of paintball!" He reassured me and gave me a nuzzling kiss on the cheek and down my neck.

"Let's hope so. You're not as young as you used to be. You've got to take good care of yourself, honey."

"Oh, so now I'm long-in-the-tooth. Go ahead and order me a Hover-Round while you're at it! Please, Amelia!"

"Oh, Shane, quit! That's not what I'm saying. I just worry about you," I gently smacked his chest, becoming exasperated with him. I was about done with my tea and still needed to pack a few outfits for the weekend.

"I think Jonesborough needs to worry with the likes of the four of you headed there! They have no idea what's about to hit the fan!" He was grinning ear-to-ear like a Cheshire cat. How well he knew our foursome.

"I don't know what you are referring to. We are simply going to help a friend and have some spa therapy in the process."

"There's nothing simple about any of you. Come here and give me something to remember my beautiful wife by!" he said and wrapped me in a warm embrace. "Come home soon, sweetie. I'll miss you." He swept his lips across mine in a heartfelt kiss.

"Oh, I will. I'll be home before long. You won't even miss me!"

FIVE

"I can't begin to tell you how much I appreciate everything you girls are doing to help me!" Lucy told us as we were seated around a large round table enjoying a salad and her new soup of the day, wild rice and mushroom. The tea room was buzzing with activity and nearly every table was filled. Lyla's didn't seem to be losing business with the exit of Chef Paul.

"The sorority girls came by this afternoon and my niece gave them a tour of the kitchen set up and a run through. They are going to work out great." She seemed composed and much calmer than yesterday afternoon. It's amazing what a difference a day can make!

"I'm glad!" Sarah sighed with relief. "I feel so bad about Cheryl pumping me for information and turning around to use my advice against you."

"Honey, how could you have known what she was up to? She is a nasty woman and she had an agenda. There was no way you could have known!" Lucy reassured her. "I made sure I invited all the council members to come for a complimentary lunch today. I told them it was the launch of our new menu and I wanted to get their opinion," Lucy said quite proud of herself.

"What a great idea!" I said. "And...did they like everything?"

"They loved it! It really made me feel much better to know that the locals are enjoying the change in the menu and hopefully, the National Storytelling tourists will as well," Lucy added. "If Cheryl is going to take away my chef and servers, I'm not going down without a fight!"

"This soup is outstanding, Lucy!" Olivia said appreciatively. She wiped a drop from her chin with her napkin. "Any chance I could have some more?" Olivia looked very Santa Fe today in a hand smocked turquoise blouse and wrangler jeans. She was wearing her favorite Justin boots, but had added a little "bling" with a turquoise and silver belt and matching cuff bracelet. She seemed to be dressing much more femininely these days. Maybe Lincoln had brought that out in her.

"Olivia, control yourself!" Cassandra chided her. She was dressed in a chic sapphire blue suede jacket and chocolate brown slacks. She oozed class from her perfectly cut chin length platinum blonde bob to her brown Chanel kidskin gloves and matching purse. No wonder she was always on Dogwood Cove's "Best Dressed List!"

"Please excuse Olivia, Lucy. She has a ferocious appetite!" Cassandra apologized.

"Well, Cassandra, when something is this good, you can't help but want more!" Olivia said defensively. "Is this on your new menu?" She continued to scrape the very last drop of soup from her bowl, smiling hopefully for a second helping.

"Well, I haven't quite decided on everything, but your Chef from Reynolds's has come up with some wonderful suggestions such as a daily soup of the day. He also suggested that we put some authentic British entrees on the menu such as 'toad in the hole' and 'bubble and squeak' as well as shepherd's pie to have an authentic British lunch menu."

"'Toad in the hole?' 'Bubble and squeak?' I don't think I want to know what's in that!" Olivia exclaimed. She pushed her soup bowl away from her and look horrified.

"Honey, 'toad in the hole' is just sausage baked in a pastry. 'Bubble and squeak' is cabbage and fried potatoes. It's really very tasty," Cassandra laughed at Olivia's reaction.

"I like the British Pub food idea," I said turning towards Lucy. "You could really get quite a following with the locals with that type of fare."

"I love the idea!" Sarah agreed. She looked sweet today dressed in a green and navy tartan style skirt with a solid navy hand knit cable sweater and matching tights. Her tam perched on top of her head made her look like a preppy school girl. She had dressed the part on such a cool fall afternoon.

The door was flung open as a brisk autumn wind blew fallen leaves into the entry way. We all shivered and turned to see a very thin woman dressed in black from head to toe standing in the doorway. Her over-processed peroxide blonde bangs peeked out from a black silk turban tied around her head and large dark sunglasses obscured her eyes, very Jackie Onasis.

Her hot pink lips were pursed tightly. She quickly scanned the room, removing her oversized glasses to adjust to the dim lighting. Her target in her sights, she quickly made a bee line towards our table and flung her long black wrap around her neck with one quick dramatic motion for effect. She reminded me a bit of Gloria Swanson, a famous actress from the black and white silent movie era.

"Oh, good gravy! It's Cheryl!" Sarah gasped. "What is she doing here?"

"You are not welcome here, Cheryl!" Lucy said and quickly rose from her seat. The ladies seated by the door turned towards Lucy and sat with their mouths hanging open.

"Oh, don't worry, Lucy. I won't be staying long. I just came by to tell you that I have it on good authority that I've got tonight's vote from the historic board in the bag. We'll be opening next week, just in time for the National Story Telling Festival." She was smirking now and clearly enjoyed inflicting pain on Lucy.

"It's not over until the 'Fat Lady Sings!' " Lucy informed her. "The board needs to hear how unethical you have been by hiring my chef and my wait staff. The last thing we need in Jonesborough is a new business owner who is going to go around slitting throats!"

Cheryl placed her hands on her hips, her four inch pumps making her tower over Lucy, simply dressed in khaki pants, a button down shirt, and calico apron in comparison to Cheryl's expensive looking designer outfit. "I've got your chef, I've got your servers and I've got your recipes. I give you a month before you close your doors for good!" she threatened.

"Cheryl, I had no idea your intentions were so underhanded! I don't think Jake and his parents have any idea how deceitful you have been in plotting against Lyla's," Sarah said as she jumped up to Lucy's defense. "You used me to get information. I had no idea you were planning on buying a building directly across Main Street from Lyla's and putting in your own tea room!" Sarah was furious, her hands balled into fists. Her tam was trembling ever so slightly on top of her head.

"All's fair in love and war, Sarah my dear!" Cheryl said as she brushed by her. "You are about as naive as Snow White!" she sneered and continued circling the table.

"And you are about as ruthless as Snow White's evil stepmother! And let's remember, she didn't have much of a storybook ending!" Olivia snapped. "Can't you come up with an original idea for your business? Why do you have to open a tea room? Why Lucy's chef? Why her recipes?"

"And you are… ?" Cheryl asked sarcastically, looking Olivia up and down in a condescending manner.

"Lucy's loyal friend and I'm not about to let you or anyone else destroy this woman or this business. Lyla's is an institution in Jonesborough. When people find out what you are trying to do, you will be the one closing your doors in a month!" Olivia informed her.

"Well between my new women's boutique in the Salt House and the new dinner theatre I'm opening in the Parson's Table, I'd say I pretty much have Jonesborough in my back pocket. Lyla's will be a distant memory and I'll be running this town. What the heck! I may as well run for Mayor!"

"I've seen your kind before," Cassandra said and rose from her seat to face Cheryl. "Bad girl from the wrong side of the tracks hooks the big fish. You may think because you wear designer now instead of off-the-rack that you are really somebody, but at the end of the day, you've still got to look in the mirror and live with yourself. What you are doing to Lucy just shows that just because you have money, doesn't mean you have an ounce of class."

Olivia rose from her chair, straightening her back, her petite five foot frame ram rod stiff. "Now if you'll excuse us, this is a private party. Please leave! Good day!"

"Well, I never!" Cheryl said and turned on her heel. "This is not the last you've heard of me, Lucy Lyle!" She called over her shoulder. She stomped a path across the hardwood floor, threw the door open and headed into the turbulent wind. The door slammed behind her as a flurry of dried leaves settled to the floor.

"What the heck just happened?" I asked stunned.

"'Cruella Deville' lives on!" Lucy snorted.

"Lucy, you were right with your description," I told her. "Well the meeting starts in a half an hour. Gosh, it's already dark outside! We had better head over soon to be sure to get a seat," I reminded everyone.

"I feel like I need a bath after being around her!" Olivia said as she rubbed her arms. "It's going to be fine, Lucy. We've got your back! Boy, it feels like the temperature has dropped!"

We all hurriedly cleared the table and took our dishes to the kitchen sanitation area. We gathered near the front door and I pulled on my trusty London Fog black trench coat. It was a wardrobe 'must have' and looked nice tonight with my tailored black wool slacks and heather gray turtleneck. I turned the collar up to buffer the brisk wind that was blowing leaves all over the sidewalks on Main Street.

"I'll just tell Darla to lock up for tonight," Lucy said as she began taking off her apron. "What's the famous quote Scarlett O'Hara said? 'Tomorrow is another day?'" Lucy laughed and shook her head. "Good night, Darla! See you in the morning," Lucy called out to her niece as she walked across the original worn floors towards the front door.

"Good night, Aunt Lucy! Bundle up. It's going to be a cold night!" Darla called from the kitchen door. "And good luck tonight!"

"Thanks, Darla dear!" Lucy said and began putting on her black wool cape and fastened the hook in front at the nape of her neck. She pulled the attached hood up over her head to buffer herself from the wind.

"It sure is chilly tonight," Sarah commented rubbing her hands together.

"And look at that fog rolling in," Olivia added. "It makes Jonesborough look a bit like *Sleepy Hollow.*"

"What a creepy night!" Cassandra said. "I'll be glad to get over to the Carnegie and get some hot stone therapy. This kind of damp and chilly night gets in your bones!"

We were all glad the courthouse was just across the street from Lyla's as the fog continued to roll in. It was one of those nights that strangely resembled a Hollywood movie scene. But that did not deter the town folk of Jonesborough from attending the meeting. We could tell that there would be a full house by the dozens of people walking up the courthouse steps and several groups of locals standing about talking. Something was definitely in the air tonight!

We quickly crossed Main Street and scurried up the courthouse steps. We followed the crowd into the largest courtroom that served as the meeting room for the historical board. The rows of seats were quickly filling and it looked like there would be standing room only by the time the meeting started in just about twenty more minutes.

"Here are six seats together. We'll save one for Imogene," Lucy gestured. She seemed much more confident this evening. I'm sure the meeting with the new chef had been a shot in the arm. I was glad to see she was excited about the new menu. Sometimes adversity can force one to make changes that are actually good for growth. Maybe Lucy would benefit from Chef Paul leaving. She might not have ever thought of changing her menu. We began unbuttoning our coats and getting settled for the night's events.

"Oh, golly! I need to go back and tell Darla to unplug the space heaters for tonight," Lucy informed us. "I'll be right back. It shouldn't take but a minute. Not all of these old buildings are up to the new fire codes," Lucy informed us. "The last thing I need right now is a fire."

"Go on, Lucy. We'll save your seat," Sarah reassured her and laid her navy blue pea coat across Lucy's vacant chair.

The historical board members were slowly filling in their seats that were configured in an elevated semi-circle facing the audience. There were a total of six members and I recognized a few of the faces. There was Pete Johnson that owned Main Street Pharmacy, a business that had been in his family for close to 200 years. Ruth Gordon who owned Ruthie's Sweet Shop was seated to his right. She was a client of ours and carried a selection of our Smoky Mountain Coffees along with Reynolds's Candies and other wonderful homemade desserts. Ruthie's was a popular late night hang out following the Jonesborough Repertory Theatre productions and by all accounts was doing a brisk business. I wondered what Cheryl's dinner theatre would do to their bottom line? I waved at Ruthie who seemed pleasantly surprised to see me.

"Whoo Hoo! Girls!" Imogene called out as she made her grand entrance. Tonight she was decked out in a black and white zebra inspired number, from her swing coat and blouse to her pumps and handbag. She was proudly wearing her rather enormous Joan Rivers black jett ring and matching bangle bracelets, straight from QVC. You had to admire Aunt Imogene. She was no shrinking violet!

"Did I miss the fireworks yet?" She began air kissing greetings to each of us as she slid down the row of chairs to take her seat.

"Imogene, I love the zebra. Where did you find this great outfit?" Sarah said in awe.

"Well, Stein Mart was having a blow-out sale and you know I can't pass up a good deal. I'm not sure why someone else didn't snatch this up, but their loss is my gain!" She grinned and began surveying the room. "Hey Elizabeth, hey Joel!" She yelled and waved a white handkerchief wildly about above her head.

"Don't say a word that I told you this," she said as she whispered in my ear, "but Elizabeth Evans over there has just had some major plastic surgery done. She told everyone she was having an appendectomy but from what I heard, it was more like a tummy tuck, eyebrow lift and boob job." She shook her head slowly, up and down. That was Imogene. First to know all the juicy details. "Poor Joel," she continued. "He doesn't have a clue that she's been fooling around with her plastic surgeon."

"Aunt Imogene!" I admonished her and slapped at her hand.

"What? It's true! I heard about it when I picked up Fiona from the dog groomer's. Elizabeth's housekeeper had just been in to pick up her Irish Setter and told Suzy."

"I don't want to know anymore," I said shaking my head. Oh, if these people only knew how much of their personal lives was discussed amongst the town folk. *Who would have thought such a small town could hold so many secrets?*

"Excuse me," Lucy said to the people in our row as she squeezed past their knees and heavy coats in their laps. "That fog is thicker than pea soup," she whispered loudly to us as she took her seat.

"This meeting is called to order," Pete Johnson said into the microphone as he pounded the gavel. "Please take your seats and come to order." He paused and looked around the room as a hush fell on the standing room only audience.

"First order of business is the permit to open a restaurant for Mrs. Cheryl White. Mrs.White, please approach the podium," Pete requested into the microphone.

"Where is she?" Olivia asked loudly. "I don't see the 'Dragon Lady.' Maybe she missed the meeting." Several people in the row in front of us turned to look inquisitively at Olivia.

"Olivia, hush!" Cassandra hissed. "People can hear you!"

A murmur began at the back of the room as everyone waited for Cheryl to come forward.

"Mrs. White. Has anyone seen Mrs. Cheryl White?" Pete spoke loudly into the microphone. He paused for a few moments. The murmuring grew louder as more and more time passed and still no Cheryl.

"All right, we will move to our next order of business,"

Pete said into the microphone which quieted the room. "The placement of a historical marker in the town square."

The double side doors were flung open as a breathless man burst into the room.

"Sheriff, Sheriff! Come quickly!" He yelled. "There's been a murder on the Andrew Jackson Bridge."

"A murder? Oh, my heavens!" Aunt Imogene exclaimed grabbing her cell phone.

The East River Bridge was built in the 1880's and was later renamed the Andrew Jackson Bridge in honor of Jonesborough's most famous resident, Old Hickory himself, who practiced law and acted as judge when Jonesborough was a rough and young territory. The bridge intersects the Nolichucky River and is one of the few covered bridges remaining in the United States. It has been photographed in many books spotlighting the history of Appalachia and has been featured on Bill Landry's Emmy award winning Heartland Series. The bridge was positioned just east of the Jonesborough Courthouse.

Sheriff Anderson quickly moved through the crowd towards the doors. He motioned for a deputy and got on his radio. Another deputy entered from the outer hallway and spoke quietly with Sheriff Anderson.

"Folks, please keep your seats. We don't want anyone interfering with our investigation. All of you must remain inside until we've had a chance to question you. Deputy Barnes will be securing this room and I'm asking all of you to remain cooperative as this might take a while. He closed the double doors behind him and Deputy Barnes took his position, one hand on his pistol handle, the other, tucked into his belt. He resembled Barney Fife and I couldn't help myself. I got tickled as I watched him pace back and forth in front of the double doors.

The historical board members had left their chairs and were milling about with the crowd. Aunt Imogene was on the phone with one of her real estate associates, telling them the latest news. She always enjoyed out scooping her friends. This time she was in the middle of all the action.

"Yes, yes that's what the sheriff said—a *MURDER!* Yes indeed! The Andrew Jackson Bridge, the covered bridge right past the Jonesborough Courthouse." She grabbed a bag of peanuts from her purse and began eating them. "I'll call you back when I know more. Good idea! I'll tweet about it. Bye!" she quickly hung up her cell phone and gave the peanuts her full attention.

"Since when did you start tweeting?" I asked her, amused.

"You mean you don't use Twitter?" She asked me, shocked.

"I try not to. Who has the time?"

"It's great for business and you can keep all your contacts up-to-date with the latest," she said with authority.

"Yeah, like Jessica Simpson just had her roots touched up," Olivia smirked.

"Quit!" Cassandra elbowed her.

"You have any more peanuts, Imogene?" Olivia asked. She looked over at Cassandra, an amused smile across her face. "Well, we may be here a while. I've got to keep up my strength and after all, I did not get to have a second bowl of soup. That was a very lite dinner for me." She crossed her arms and leaned back in her chair.

"Oh, Olivia. You'll survive!" Cassandra retorted.

"I know where there is a vending machine downstairs," Imogene informed her. "They have cookies, chips, candy bars… All the major brands."

"Where downstairs?" Olivia perked up with the good news.

"Hey. Didn't you hear what the sheriff said?" I asked her. "No one leaves this room until we are all questioned and I think "Deputy-Do-Right" means business!"

"Well, there's got to be some law about detaining us without bathroom privileges and some kind of sustenance," Olivia grumbled.

"Good grief, Olivia. It's been less than five minutes. You'll live!" Cassandra snapped. "I think we should be thinking more about the poor soul who lost their life on the bridge and less about our stomachs right now!"

"You're right, you're right. But seriously, I hope they do make some arrangements if we are going to be here long." Olivia stood up and began looking towards the windows.

"It looks like they are examining some sort of Lexus sedan by the bridge," she said struggling to stand on her toes to see out the window that was just a bit too high for her small stature.

Aunt Imogene, not to be left out of the investigation, stood up and pushed through the crowd towards the window. "What color Lexus, Olivia?" Imogene questioned.

"It looks like it might be tan or maybe metallic. I'm not sure," Olivia admitted.

"Is it a gold Lexus?" Lucy asked, her face losing some of its color.

"Yeah. A gold Lexus," Imogene reported. She quickly began texting her contacts with the update.

"Does it have Florida tags?" Lucy asked, still seated.

"Hmm. Let's see. I'm not sure." She reached into her zebra hand bag and dug around for what seemed like an eternity. She rustled through papers, check books, and ziplock baggies full of what-nots, until she was victorious. She proudly removed a set of binoculars. She held them up to her eyes and quickly got a bead on the crime scene

"You carry binoculars?" I said in disbelief. "How big IS your handbag? It's like a magic show where the magician pulls out a palm tree from his top hat," I teased her.

"You never know what you will need and when something will come in handy!" she snipped back at me. "If that Sheriff would just move a couple of inches, I could see. There! Yep, Florida tags." More quick and furious typing on her touchpad phone.

"It's Cheryl's car," Lucy said, her voice flat and void of emotion.

"Oh, no!" Sarah gasped. "Do you think Cheryl is the one who was murdered?"

"It looks that way," said Imogene. "Who would do such a terrible thing?"

"This isn't the first murder that has happened on that same bridge," Sarah said suddenly serious. "There was a couple killed there in the 1940's."

"Yes there was," Imogene agreed with Sarah. "It still remains one of the area's most famous unsolved murders.

"What murder? Who are you talking about?" Olivia spun away from the window and asked Sarah.

"The Andrew Jackson Bridge Murders," Sarah said, her eyes as big as saucers. "It was a night, just like tonight—a thick fog had enveloped the area and it was hard to see a thing!"

"Okay. So when was this? I don't remember hearing about a couple being murdered in this area," Olivia remarked.

"It was the late 1940's," Imogene informed her. "I remember it vividly because everyone was afraid to go out at night for a long time after Patrick Dover and Julie Beatty were killed. Daddy used to have to drive my beaux home because of the Andrew Jackson Bridge murders."

"But what happened?" Olivia asked, beginning to sound exasperated.

"Patrick and Julie were having a romantic moment on the covered bridge. It was the famous spot for young lovers back in the day," Imogene said wistfully. "I remember when Phillip Osgood took me for a drive and parked by the bridge," Imogene gushed. "Phillip was so handsome. Many a young girl would have gladly traded places with me!"

"Aunt Imogene! I didn't know you dated Mr. Osgood," I teased her.

"That was a life time ago and many boyfriends ago. In fact I remember many a hot summer night by the bridge."

"Imogene, before you go any further down memory lane, back to what happened to Patrick and Julie," Olivia reminded her.

"Yes, yes! Back to Patrick," Imogene said moving her head side to side as if to clear her thoughts. "Julie was able to tell a nurse shortly before she passed away at the hospital. What she told her was quite frightening!" she said, pausing to read an incoming text on her phone.

"Imogene! You're killing me!" Olivia whined. "Stop texting and tell us the story," she pleaded.

"Sorry, Olivia! I've got people wanting updates as to what is going on. Where was I?"

"Julie told the nurse at the hospital something frightening…" I reminded her.

"Yes, yes! Just as she and Patrick decided to head home, they noticed a dark shadow walking across the bridge toward them. Julie assumed it was another couple, but was soon surprised by a large man dressed in a black cape who came up to them and took an axe to Patrick!"

"Oh, how horrible!" Cassandra gasped and grabbed her pearl choker around her throat. "That poor boy!"

"What about Julie?" Olivia asked sharply. "How did she manage to get away?"

"She turned and started to run across the covered bridge, but not before he chopped her with the axe. She still managed to make it across the bridge and get help," Imogene shared with the group gathered closely around her. We were on pins and needles, hanging on her every word.

"Lucky for Julie, just as she reached the road by the Courthouse, a young couple was driving by and Julie managed to stop them for help. The couple reported later to the police that they saw a man with a bloody axe approaching their car. They floored the gas, just in time to get away. They were so startled by the hooded figure in black that they inadvertently hit him, as he jumped in front of their car. They were so frightened, they didn't dare stop, but kept going straight to the hospital," Imogene concluded.

"Poor Patrick, poor Julie!" Sarah lamented.

"Yes. Poor Julie. The police never found the body of the

hooded man the driver hit. They found no evidence of blood or anything to indicate anyone had been injured on the side of the road. It was like he just disappeared!" Imogene looked wistfully out the courthouse window towards the crime scene tape once again being wrapped around the entrance to the Andrew Jackson Bridge.

"There was no blood at all? How is that possible?" Olivia questioned Imogene.

"It's one of the area's oldest unsolved murders," Imogene informed us. "To this day, many people who have walked across the covered bridge at night have seen a young woman, covered in blood running across the bridge. Many people think it the ghost of Julie, running to get help. Each time the police go out to investigate, they have found no trace of blood or an injured woman."

"Oh how awful!" Sarah gasped. "Poor Julie's ghost is between two parallels."

"Between two what?" Olivia asked sarcastically.

"Julie cannot reach the next parallel universe until she solves her own murder as well as Patrick's." Sarah simply stated.

"Okay. Now I've heard everything! You've been watching one too many episodes of *Ghost Whisperer!* You are really starting to freak me out, Sarah!" Olivia shook her head in amazement.

"Olivia, many people have documented run-ins with ghosts. I for one have had my own personal experience with a ghost on campus at the University of Tennessee library," she said shaking her head in the affirmative.

"Okay, so now you're telling me that UT is haunted? I've heard it all!" Olivia scoffed.

"It's true!" Sarah cried out defensively. "Ask any of the librarians or the students who have had to study in the stacks at the James D. Hoskins Library!"

"What do you mean by stacks, Sarah honey?" Cassandra asked in a soothing voice.

"The stacks are behind the reference section. That's where they used to store all the outdated volumes. Occasionally a research student will need access to the old books to work on their thesis. It's located in the basement section of the library."

"Sounds creepy already," I agreed with Sarah and rubbed the goose bumps on my arms.

"And when did this run-in with a ghost happen, Nancy Drew?" Olivia mocked her.

"Quit teasing Sarah," Cassandra chastised and smacked Olivia's arm. "I'm listening, Sarah. You've got my curiosity aroused."

"Well, it was my senior year at The University of Tennessee and I was finishing up my history credit. My research paper was on the founding of the Lost State of Franklin, a topic I still find very fascinating to this day."

"Lost State of Franklin? What is that a spin-off of *The Land of The Lost?*" Olivia teased good naturedly.

"No, Olivia!" Sarah shot back. "The Lost State of Franklin was a territory created in 1784 with Jonesborough as its capital. It was a region offered by North Carolina to help pay off its debts from the Revolutionary War. It fell two votes short of admission as the fourteenth state and would have been called Frankland."

"Wow! I had no idea! Sarah, I apologize for teasing you," Olivia said sincerely, giving her a hug. "Did anyone else know she was the 'brainiac' in the group?" Olivia joked and quickly hugged her again.

"Okay, enough of the history lesson. Back to the stacks," Cassandra reminded Sarah.

"Yes. I was doing research in the stacks at the Hoskins Library when I felt as if someone was watching me over my shoulder! But when I turned around, no one was there. I chalked it up to an over-active imagination. You know how musty and dimly lit those old library basements can be!" she eagerly admitted.

"But I thought you said you had a run-in with a ghost," I said feeling a bit disappointed.

"I did! I needed to go during fall break and the campus was basically deserted. I went to the stacks for an article on the South West Territory that would later become Tennessee and that's when I saw her!" she exclaimed.

"Saw who?" Cassandra gasped.

"The ghost of Fay McNeil," Sarah whispered.

"Who? Who is Fay McNeil?" Cassandra asked.

" Fay McNeil was the head librarian in 1911. She was the sister-in-law of President Taylor."

"How do you know it was her?" Olivia skeptically inquired.

"I've actually seen her picture hanging in the library. I saw her ghost in the stacks. Her hair was pulled back in a severe bun and was wearing a bustled dress from that time period. It had to be her! She brushed right past me with her finger held up to her mouth as if she were telling me to be quiet."

"Sarah I think the moldy old books must have gone to your brain!" Olivia said flippantly. "You expect me to believe that you saw a woman wearing a bustle in the stacks of the library and she was floating around telling you to be quiet? I've heard it all!" she snickered and rolled her eyes.

"Fine! Don't believe me, Olivia! I know what I saw and I'm not the only one!" She adjusted her sweater and crossed her arms for added emphasis. "There have been many documentations of people studying in the stacks and seeing the ghost of Fay and no one else has been downstairs with them."

"Of course not!" Olivia jeered. "Then there would be witnesses to this paranormal activity. I think maybe the glue from the book bindings have gone to everyone's heads, that's what I think!"

"Olivia, haven't you read all the books that have been published about hauntings in East Tennessee?" I asked her. "Sarah isn't the only one who has seen ghosts on the campus of U.T."

"Et tu, Amelia? What are you? A card caring member of *Ghost Busters* now?" Olivia said sarcastically.

"You really should read one of the books. Whether you believe in ghosts or not, it gives you some background history on our region. The stories are quite fascinating!"

"Girls, it looks like the coroner has arrived," Imogene stated as she peered out the window with her binoculars. "I'm going to call Jared Roberts and see if he has an I.D. on the body," she said and turned her back as she dialed a phone number on her cell phone.

"Your Aunt has the coroner's office on speed dial?" Olivia remarked. "That's kind of creepy!"

"I guess you never know when it will come in handy in certain situations," I said and shrugged my shoulders.

"Do you think they already have an I.D. this early?" Cassandra asked skeptically.

"In a small town like this, everyone knows everyone and everything. Somebody is bound to have identified the body by now," I murmured looking around the room at the spectators standing around the windows. "Someone in here knows what happened."

"At the least, they have already run the tags on the car and checked the vic's wallet for confirmation of an I.D.," Sarah surmised.

"What's with the police lingo? Vic's?" Olivia mocked Sarah.

"Vic's as in victim's," Sarah retorted.

"You sound like a groupie of *Dog The Bounty Hunter*. You watch way to much TV, Sarah," Olivia laughed and bumped her hit playfully into Sarah's side. "You know I love you though, right?"

"It's definitely Cheryl White," Imogene announced to the room and anyone else who might be listening within two miles of the court house. "Jared Roberts, my contact at the coroner's office, just confirmed her identity," she continued as a murmur went around the room.

"Poor Cheryl," Sarah sighed and sat down. "I probably should call Jake and tell him the bad news myself. It would be better if he heard it from me."

"I'm sorry I was so hard on you, Sarah," Olivia said and sat in the seat next to her. She put her arm protectively around her shoulders. "This has got to be difficult for you."

"I really only met Cheryl the one time, but I feel terrible for the White's. How is this going to affect Jake and his family?"

"And I feel terrible as well," Lucy admitted and leaned

down to hug Sarah. "I said some awful things about Cheryl and I hate to think that she spent her final moments arguing with me."

"Lucy—this is not your fault! Your business was under attack!" I reminded her. "You did what you had to do to keep your doors open. You did not bring this on Cheryl!"

"Amelia's right, Lucy," Cassandra agreed. "Cheryl is the one who instigated the feud between the two of you. When it comes to your business, you've got to stand up and fight for what is right and fair! I've had competitors try to obtain our recipes. You've got to protect what you've worked so hard to achieve. No one can blame you for that!"

"I know. I know you are right, girls! But I still feel awful about Cheryl. Who would be so cold blooded as to murder her?" Lucy asked perplexed.

Who indeed? There was a room full of suspects and possibly among us, a killer!

SIX

I slept fitfully through the night, having recurring nightmares. A woman dressed in a black turban and dark sunglasses was chasing me around the study area of the stacks. It was a relief to look around the bedroom and see that morning was breaking. Our suite at The Carnegie Hotel was very refined with rooms furnished with cherry sleigh beds, large soaking tubs, and luxurious terry cloth robes. It was an elegant addition to the Johnson City area and I loved the charm of the 1800's the hotel exuded.

I dragged myself to take a hot shower and wash some of last night's drama away. We all had been questioned individually by deputies and it had taken quite some time to explain what each of had been doing in Jonesborough and why we had attended the meeting. We did not even return to the hotel until somewhere around eleven thirty in the evening. Exhausted by the day's events, we had all said good night and headed quickly to our beds.

I walked into the living room of our suite and was surprised to see Sarah already up and about. She was dressed in a red silk Chinese jacket paired with black ankle length tapered pants and ballet flats. She had twisted her brunette hair up and secured it with chopsticks. Very chic!

"Konnichiha, Sarah!" I teased bending at the waist in a reverent bow. "You're up early!"

"Konnichiha, Amelia." She was pouring green tea into a white tea cup. "Would you care for some Japanese Sencha this morning?"

"Absolutely. Thank you," I paused as she filled my tea cup. "Sarah, how is Jake's family handling the news?"

"Well, understandably, they are quite upset. They will be arriving in Jonesborough sometime this morning." She took a sip of her tea and stared down at her lap.

"How are you Sarah?" I walked over to the loveseat and sat next to her.

"I can't help but feel terrible even though I didn't know her well. My heart is breaking for Jake and his parents." She continued taking small sips of her tea, comforting herself in the process.

"And how are things between you and Jake?" I gently asked, rubbing her back for support. I was never sure with Sarah because she was such a private person. She seemed more content with helping everyone else rather than burdening anyone with her own problems.

"Right now, I'm not even sure. We are giving it a go, but there have been a few bumps in the road," she smiled gently and continued. "Quite frankly, Jake is just too much of a 'mama's boy' and has to first run everything by her. I refuse to compete with his mom."

Wow, this was the most she had ever said about her relationship!

"Jake White is a 'mama's boy?' That doesn't seem to fit with the 'roving reporter' stereotype," I told her.

"Well, I've been trying to encourage him to apply for a job with *The Knoxville News Sentinel*. Jake is a phenomenal reporter and he has outgrown *The Dogwood Daily*. I think he could really end up being an award winning investigative reporter," Sarah said and smiled at me, looking quite pleased with her man!

"Sounds like you are his number one fan! Jake is lucky to have someone so supportive of his career," I told her.

"I am supportive of him! I realize if Jake gets a job with a bigger paper, he will have to move. But, that's how much I believe in him. I want to see him succeed!" She had a very determined look on her face and I could tell how much she loved him.

"And Jake's Mom?" I inquired. I had a feeling what she was going to tell me.

"Jake is an only child and he has a lot of pressure from his parents to stay close by in Dogwood Cove. I'm almost sure Mrs. White would be happy if Jake moved back home." It was evident Sarah was frustrated!

"Don't get me wrong. I love the White's. I just think in her mind, no one is good enough for Jake." Sarah's lower lip trembled and she nearly toppled the teacup in her lap. "Whoops! I guess I need to steady my nerves."

"Why didn't you tell me about this before, Sarah?" I took her hand and looked her in the eye. "Everyone needs someone to talk to. You know, I went through the same thing with Shane's Mom when we started dating. She was very protective of her little boy," I revealed.

"But you and Mrs. Spencer are so close. I never would have guessed you two had ever had any issues."

"Well, I just had to show her that I loved Shane as much as she did and once she realized that, she gave us her blessing. She just didn't want to feel as though she was losing Shane. I think it's hard for Moms when their sons become serious about a woman," I concluded and poured each of us some more tea.

"I see what you are saying. Maybe I need to stop looking at Jake's Mom as competition and take some of the pressure off of him." She was nodding her head in agreement. "I've been contributing to the problem. I guess I've been making him feel like he's had to make a choice."

"Well, most likely he's getting pressure from his Mom as well." I took a sip of tea and continued, "I remember making a beautiful dinner for Shane and the Spencer's when we had been dating for about three months and all Mrs. Spencer did was compare my macaroni and cheese to hers, how her pie crust was always homemade, never store-bought shortcuts, and how Shane really didn't like meatloaf even though he was gobbling down mine. She was very competitive to show me she knew Shane best," I laughed thinking back to that nightmarish dinner.

"How did you handle it?" she asked, surprised by my admission.

"Shane just gently squeezed my knee under the table and smiled at me. I knew he was asking me to be tolerant of his mom and because I loved him, I didn't act like it bothered me. And you know—he loves my meatloaf! He just doesn't like his Mom's because she puts green pepper and onions in it." We both started laughing at the absurdity of competing over meatloaf! It did seem silly.

"Oh, I feel much better, Amelia. Thank you!" Sarah hugged me tightly.

"Feel better about what? What did I miss?" Olivia inquired. "Has anyone ordered room service?"

"I ordered some Japanese Sencha green tea. Would you like a cup?" Sarah offered.

"I would," Cassandra said making a grand entrance in a black pant suit with red patent leather pumps and matching handbag. She looked like she had walked out of a Parisian salon.

"I'm starving. Where's the room service menu?" Olivia asked and began searching the desk drawers.

"I know of a great place for breakfast and it's a pretty country drive—The Farmer's Daughter on the way to Greeneville. They serve a family style breakfast and lunch on the weekends," I said to the group.

"Well, let's load up, then!" Olivia perked up. "I'll grab my jacket and let's go!" She put on a beautiful tan suede duster and looked the part of a cowgirl with her chocolate brown ostrich boots, dark denim jeans and pumpkin colored suede shirt cinched smartly at the waist with a matching chocolate brown ostrich belt. She had really "upped" her fashion selections. Cassandra had been a good influence on her, even though she had been so reluctant at first to improve her style.

"If you don't mind riding in "Ladybug" I'll drive," I offered.

"No offense, Amelia. But I feel somewhat claustrophobic in your clown car," Olivia whined.

"Well, Olivia. Not everyone enjoys riding around in a mud covered monster truck. I don't know how you can even climb up in that big cab. It's ridiculous!" Cassandra quipped.

"It's a farm truck. It has to be big to haul horse trailers and loads of hay," Olivia said and turned towards me. "Sorry, Amelia! I didn't mean to sound insulting. I just need coffee and a big breakfast."

"And a big muzzle." Cassandra added. "I'll drive, Amelia, if that is all right with Queen Sheba over here."

"Can I sit up front with the seat warmers?" Olivia asked excited at the prospect of riding in Cassandra's Mercedes.

"I thought you said seat warmers were for elitists!" Cassandra reminded her.

"That's before I used your seat warmers. I'm thinking of having some put in my next truck."

We all laughed and walked out to the elevator. As we waited for the doors to open, my cell phone rang. Expecting it to be Shane and the kids, I immediately answered it.

"Good morning!"

"Not for me, it's not!" Lucy complained on the other end. "I've been summoned to the Jonesborough police department for questioning in Cheryl's murder."

"What? It's Lucy. She's been asked to come to the police station for questioning," I told the group. The elevator doors opened and we all stepped on for the descent to the lobby.

"Tell her it's time to hire an attorney," Cassandra advised.

"Lucy. Do you have an attorney?" I quickly asked.

"Yes. Do you think I need an attorney? Oh, my goodness! This is becoming a nightmare!"

"Keep your head collected, Lucy. Call your attorney and have them meet you at the station. Don't talk without your attorney, okay?"

"Okay, I'm calling right now. Thanks, Amelia!"

"Is Lyla's open today?"

"Yeah, but I have the new chef and my niece Darla running things. The sorority girls are also scheduled to come in, so I think everything is under control."

"Call us when you are headed to the station. We'll meet you there and help figure all this out," I reassured her.

"You're a good friend, Amelia. I don't know how I would have gotten through this without you.

"Hang in there, Lucy!" I quickly snapped the cell phone closed.

"I think we better get something quick to eat and table The Farmer's Daughter for another day," I announced. "Lucy will need us at the police station. Should we grab a quick bite to eat here at the hotel?"

"Isn't there a Pal's two parking lots up from here?" Olivia asked with excitement in her voice. "I think I noticed that last night when we came home so late. I could go for a country ham biscuit right now."

"Olivia, the bottomless pit!" Cassandra teased.

"Hey! You know as well as I that questioning at the police department can take a lot of time. If there's one thing I know from dating Lincoln, you've got to be sharp and on your toes. Food helps me focus!" Olivia replied, a bit defensively.

"I think you've missed your calling, Liv. You should take over Guy Fieri's job on Food Network and start hosting *Diners, Drive-ins And Dives*." Cassandra was laughing as we swung around the bright blue building and placed our order at the window.

Some things never change. Unfortunately for Lucy, her circumstances were going to change—and for the worse.

SEVEN

"Oh girls, there you are!" Lucy said and took her time hugging each of us. "Lewis Franks, my attorney," she said as a means of introduction to the group.

"Ladies, good morning," Mr. Franks said warmly. "I'm sure this will not take too long. We'll get this little matter of an alibi taken care of straight away," he said as he winked, his syllables stretched out in a long southern drawl. "This should be very open and shut as far as I'm concerned and you ladies were all with Mrs. Lyle when she last saw the victim." He was starting to sound a bit like Boss Hog from *The Dukes of Hazzard*. I inwardly hoped he was a better attorney than what he appeared to be on the surface.

"Not so open and shut from what I hear," a voice piped up from behind the group. "Mr. Franks, I'm Detective Deakins. If you'll follow me, Mrs. Lyle, I would like to ask you a few questions regarding your conversation with the victim prior to the meeting at the courthouse. Please follow me," he instructed brusquely.

"Lucy is the victim here, Detective Deakins. A victim of Cheryl White's greed and she was with us all afternoon before we went to the courthouse," Olivia spoke up. "You might as well question all of us."

"I intend to do just that. Thank you," he said sarcastically. "You saved me a phone call. Ladies, have a seat," he said and motioned to the chairs in the waiting area. "This may be a while." He walked briskly with Lucy and Lewis Franks in tow, struggling along to keep up with him.

"You and your big mouth, Olivia!" Cassandra fussed at her.

"'Go ahead and question all of us!'" she said loudly and mimicked Olivia. "You've been watching too many episodes of *Law and Order*. I could just pinch your head off!" she shouted with her fists up in the air.

"I'm calling Lincoln. He'll get this straightened out." Olivia pulled out her cell phone and began punching in his number.

"He'll tell you the same thing. Just because you date a cop doesn't mean you get a pass on this one," Cassandra said knowingly.

"It's just going straight to voicemail. I'll try him later," Olivia said discouraged.

"Well, while we are here, we've got to figure out who has motive to want Cheryl dead. Lucy wasn't the only one in town with an axe to grind with her," I said emphatically.

"We could start a list of people who might be upset about her recent real estate purchases," Sarah suggested.

"Okay. Let's start there," I agreed. "I would begin with her two stepdaughters. They couldn't have been too happy that she was spending all of their Dad's money on real estate. After all, they are contesting the will, right Sarah?"

"Right, yes you're right!" Sarah agreed.

"What about shopkeepers?" I asked on a roll. "I would think the Jonesborough Repertory Theatre would be upset that

Cheryl was planning on putting a dinner theatre in the Parson's Table," I assumed.

"Genius, Amelia. And what about shopkeepers that might be unhappy regarding a women's boutique going in the Salt House?" Olivia suggested.

"Well, I'm not sure about her taste in clothes. They probably wouldn't have been too affected by that," Cassandra joked. Cassandra was *definitely* a fashion diva! She was invited to New York's Fashion Week and was seen at all the major shows in Paris as well. Cassandra was a down-to-earth Tennessee girl, but she had a reputation for being a clothes horse.

"Who else?" I wondered aloud. "Maybe there was someone else who also wanted to buy the Salt House and the Parson's Table?" I suggested. "I should call Imogene and ask what she knows."

"You won't have to, she's coming through the door," Olivia laughed, amazed at her timing.

"Imogene! What are you doing here?" I asked and exchanged a quick air kiss with her.

"Oh, well you know how gossip spreads like wildfire in a small town. One of my realtor friends saw y'all going into the police station and tweeted me."

"Are there no secrets in Jonesborough?" I asked. Imogene had gone with a black and white horizontal striped sweater and black pants today. What an appropriate top to wear to a police station. The black and white stripes slightly resembled the inmate's outfits from Elvis's *Jail House Rock* video.

"Imogene. Come sit down. I have something you might be able to help us with," I said and gestured to an uncomfortable looking bright orange plastic chair.

"That's why I came. Girls, I'm here to help," she said quickly.

"Was anyone else interested in the properties Cheryl purchased?"

"Well, yes. Both properties had been on the market for a while. I have it on good authority that Delilah Bennett had her eye on The Salt House. She wanted to open a quilt shop and antique store. She was in the process of getting her financing together. She was just a day or two away from getting approved by the bank," Imogene said thoughtfully.

"Delilah Bennett. That name sounds familiar!" Cassandra said. "Wasn't there something in the papers about her recently?"

"Yes, yes there was. You know the Bennett's. Her husband owns the gas station on the corner. He was accused of gas price fixing last year when the economy was so bad. No one was able to ever prove anything though," Imogene concluded and crossed her legs. She tapped her long red fingernails on her red bedazzled cell phone and gazed off in the distance.

"And what about the Parson's Table?" I wondered out loud.

"Now there's a story," Imogene volunteered turning her full attention towards me. "You know that restaurant critic from the paper, *The Northeast Tennessean*?" she asked me.

"Frank Dupree?" Cassandra groaned.

"Yes, that's the guy," Imogene stated. "He had put together a group of investors to finance the purchase of The Parson's Table. He said it would put Jonesborough on the culinary map. He had big plans for renovations—BIG PLANS! He had that good looking female blonde designer from HGTV commissioned to work on it. They were going to shoot some reality program about the renovations," she concluded.

"Hey isn't Frank Dupree the guy who gave such a bad review for that restaurant, Top of the Town, that they went out of business in less than a month?" Olivia recalled.

"One and the same. Cross Frank Dupree and your eating establishment will be sure to get smeared. He has that kind of influence on where people in this area eat. I've met the man on several occasions at The Taste of Dogwood Cove and some fundraisers for the ballet and the symphony, and quite honestly, I do not care for him at all," Cassandra shook her head back and forth. "He is one of the most arrogant, temperamental people I've ever met."

"He can't be more arrogant then your 'Hollyweird' friends," Olivia ribbed her.

Cassandra rubbed elbows with many of the Hollywood jet-set crowd. Reynolds's Candies was always in the Oscar goodie bags and Cassandra was always invited to movie premiers and Hollywood philanthropic fundraisers. There were rumors that her husband Doug would soon be announcing his candidacy for Governor of Tennessee.

"Much worse than my 'Hollywood friends,'" Cassandra confirmed ignoring Olivia's comment. "He is suffering from a full-blown case of short man's syndrome!"

"Short man's syndrome? I've never heard of that," Sarah remarked.

"You know, like Napoleon Bonaparte had the need to compensate for his short stature?" Olivia told Sarah.

"Just like the guys who drive the flashy sports cars to make up for their inadequacies in the bedroom…" Imogene added.

"Aunt Imogene!" I exclaimed, covering my mouth with my hand in embarrassment.

"Well, it's true. I'm simply stating a fact. None of *MY* five husbands ever felt the need to drive a Corvette or Porsche to prove their manhood."

"Imogene, you're a gal after my own heart!" Olivia laughed and hugged her. "I believe we are kindred spirits!"

"Okay, back to the Parson's Table. Imogene, how did Cheryl White end up buying it instead of Frank Dupree?"

"There was some bickering between Frank and the chef he had hired. They couldn't agree on the décor or the menu. Both of them are control freaks. In my opinion, that business relationship was as much of a disaster as the maiden voyage of *the Titanic.* The silent partners got tired of the in-fighting between the two egos and backed out of the deal completely."

"Well I imagine that losing out on that real estate deal had Frank Dupree more than a little ticked off," I concluded.

"The in-fighting gave Cheryl just enough time to swoop in and close the deal. I don't know what contacts she had with the historic board, but she had someone behind the scenes pulling strings for her. I've never seen anything approved so quickly in all my years as a real estate agent," Imogene testified.

"With Cheryl out of the way, what's to stop Frank Dupree from buying The Parson's Table?" Olivia surmised.

"You're absolutely right, Olivia," I agreed. "We've got to look into this further."

Just then Olivia's cell phone began ringing. Her ring tone was "Rodeo: Hoedown" by American composer Aaron Copeland. It made me think of the beef commercials every time I heard it!

"Hey, Lincoln. I've been trying to reach you," Olivia said

into her cell phone. "We're down here at the Jonesborough police station for questioning in last night's murder."

"I can just imagine his response now," Cassandra laughed. "Here we go again!"

"Well, do you think you could call Detective Deakins and vouch for us at least?"

"He's probably ready to string her up by her toenails about now," Cassandra continued joking. "Those two are like fire and ice!"

"They do make a wonderful couple," Sarah commented. "Not everyone has that kind of passion in their relationship," she said a bit wistfully.

"Not everyone could put up with Olivia's headstrong ways," I reminded Sarah and sat down next to her. "In order for her to have a healthy relationship, she needs to be with someone just as strong natured as herself!"

"Hear, hear, Amelia my dear!" Cassandra agreed. "Matt Lincoln is just about the only man I've met who can seem to tame our wild filly!"

"Call me back after you talk with Deakins. And thanks... I owe you one," Olivia said and snapped her phone shut.

"He's going to call the station?" I hoped. I was worrying about Lucy and what the detective was going to talk with us about.

"Yeah. He says as long as her alibi is airtight, she's got nothing to worry about. We should be done here in time to head over to help with the National Storytelling crowd. But hopefully, we can head over to Farmer's Daughter for an early lunch, right Amelia?" Olivia asked hopefully.

The Farmer's Daughter was a well-known locally owned family style eatery near historic Greeneville, Tennessee. Each table would choose two meats from the six to eight options offered each day. Favorites included their buttermilk chicken, fried catfish, steak and gravy, pork chops and barbeque ribs. Be prepared to wear loose clothing, because all the side items served were enough to make anyone full plus the endless home-made yeast rolls and cornbread! My favorites were the carrot soufflé, fried green tomatoes and cucumber tomato cornbread salad. There's something for everyone!

"I have no problem with that. Just as soon as Lucy's finished, we should be able to go!"

"I'm afraid that may be a while," Lewis Franks stated as he walked into the waiting area. "They've placed Lucy under arrest for the murder of Cheryl White."

"What? I don't believe it!" I said dropping my handbag onto the floor. "There's got to be some kind of mistake, Mr. Lewis!"

"They've got a witness who placed a hooded cloaked figure on that bridge next to Cheryl's car," he gestured by holding his hands palm up as if in a gesture of hopelessness. *Was he really going to give up that easily?*

"It's the Andrew Jackson Bridge Murderer!" Sarah gasped. "He's back!"

"So the witness saw a hooded figure at the time of the murder. What does that have to do with Lucy?" I asked Mr. Franks.

"A whole lot since Lucy was wearing a black hooded cape style coat at the Historical Board Meeting last night," Mr. Franks stated.

"Coincidence. Circumstantial evidence at best," Olivia retorted. She strode across the room, her curly auburn hair bobbing as she quickly approached Mr. Franks. "I thought you were supposed to be some sort of rock star attorney. You've practically given up on Lucy!"

"Well the murder weapon also had her fingerprints all over it," he said defensively.

"What murder weapon? This is the first mention we've heard of a murder weapon!" I exclaimed and rose from my orange chair, shocked by this bit of news.

"A serrated pie server was found plunged into the victim's jugular. She died almost instantly. I shudder to think what a horrific death that must have been," he added.

"A serrated pie server? That does NOT even sound like a murder weapon. That sounds more like one of those death by dessert mystery series," Olivia spoke up.

"There are many people who had access to Lucy's serving pieces, Mr. Franks," Cassandra informed the attorney. "Do you realize how many people pass in and out of her kitchen each day?" she challenged him. "Someone is obviously setting Lucy up."

"Well, she did have motive…" Mr. Franks stated sheepishly.

"Did you meet Mrs. White?" Sarah spoke up. "There were a lot of people around town who had business dealings with her, including Lucy's disgruntled chef, who quit to go to work for Mrs. White along with Lucy's entire wait staff. Any one of them could have had a business relationship that went bad with Mrs. White. They all had access to Lucy's silver ware. Why don't you start by questioning one of them!" Sarah strongly suggested standing toe to toe with the bumbling attorney.

"That-a-girl, Sarah!" Olivia cheered. "Sarah's right. There are a lot of people who had access to Lucy's kitchen. Any one of them could be the killer."

"Look, I handle Ms. Lyle's business affairs. I am not qualified to serve as a criminal attorney, especially in a capital case such as this," he said backing away from Sarah.

"I'd say you're not qualified! Cassandra, can't you call Thomas to represent her?" I requested.

"Look Ms…" he stuttered, his face turning red.

"Mrs. Spencer," I flatly informed him.

"Mrs. Spencer. As I was saying, Ms. Lyle does not have an airtight alibi during the time of the murder. I'm doing the best I can!"

"What do you mean she doesn't have an alibi. She was with us!" Cassandra shouted.

"We were all together at the court house," Olivia added. " We left Lyla's Tea Room together, got seats together…"

"And Lucy went back to tell Darla to unplug the space heaters as I recall," I reminded them. "She couldn't have been gone for more than seven minutes tops."

"Just enough time to walk over to Ms. White's car on the bridge, plunge the pie server into her jugular and murder her," Mr. Franks told us.

"Lucy Lyle is a kind and upstanding person! Why… why she is a pillar of the Jonesborough community," Sarah said balling her fists at her side. Her chopsticks were shaking as she attempted to control her fury. "There is no possible way she would have committed such a violent act!"

"Any kind of violent act such as plunging a pie server into

one's jugular would have resulted in blood splatter on the murder's clothes," Olivia pointed out. "Lucy came back to the meeting with not so much as a hair out of place. She was gone for just a brief few minutes. Blood splatter like that would take a while to wash off. She could not have been the one who committed the murder," Olivia beseeched him.

"Who's the Nancy Drew now?" Sarah teased Olivia.

"Point well taken," Olivia smiled back at Sarah.

"Ah, Mr. Lewis. I think we'll take it from here." Cassandra informed him. She turned toward the group of us closely clustered about Mr. Franks who looked like he could pass out at any moment. Beads of sweat were rolling down his now fuchsia colored jowls.

"That will be fine by me. Ladies…If you will so kindly allow me to depart," he motioned with his briefcase.

"By all means!" Olivia said to his retreating back side. "What kind of bozo attorney did she have in there with her anyway?"

"Apparently, not a very competent one!" Cassandra said taking her cell phone out. "Mr. Simpson, please. This is Cassandra Reynolds calling. Yes. Yes I will hold," she said into her cell phone.

"The best thing we can do for Lucy is work on that list of suspects. Aunt Imogene, I think we're going to need your help looking more into Frank Dupree and Delilah Bennett's real estate transactions," I said to her as Cassandra continued to hold.

"I will do anything to clear Lucy's name," Imogene said. "She's been good to me over the years and I love her like a sister.

There's no possible way she would have hurt Cheryl, no matter how much she was upset over the tea room."

"Well, I'm glad you feel that way because she's going to need our help more than ever to keep Lyla's open during National Storytelling Festival as well as uncover Cheryl's murderer. It sounds like the police think this is an open and shut case already," I said.

"Yeah, that's what Lincoln just told me," Olivia stated walking over to our side of the room. "They don't have any other leads and Lucy definitely had motive!"

"And so did a lot of other people in Jonesborough as well as her step-daughter. Don't forget them," I reminded her.

"And don't forget the Andrew Jackson Bridge Murderer!" Sarah whispered. "He's come back to claim another victim!"

"Okay, Angela Lansbury! Enough already!" Olivia snapped at her. "Everyone knows that there are no such things as ghosts, Sarah!"

"I wouldn't be so sure, Olivia. I'm going to do a little research of my own and get down to the bottom of this!" she vowed.

Little did we know that Sarah would uncover a plot much more evil and sinister than the Andrew Jackson Bridge Murderer! In fact Sarah was getting ready to get tangled in a web that could cost her her life!

EIGHT

"Another order of shepard's pie, Darla, and a bowl of pumpkin bisque," Olivia called back to the hustling kitchen.

"Gosh, I had no idea it is so much work running a tea room!" she grinned and continued on to take an order from another waiting table.

"Thanks for helping today with the National Storytelling crowd," I told Cassandra as she rushed past me, her hands full of pots of tea and baskets of scones. "Lucy will be glad that Lyla's Tea Room is doing well in her absence. She has much more on her mind right now!"

"I should have packed more practical shoes," Cassandra complained aloud. "I think we will have to do a little spa therapy this evening to pamper ourselves after today's lunch crowd." Cassandra had worn one of Lucy's aprons over her Armani black jersey wool dress. Her Jimmy Choo boots with four inch stiletto heels looked fabulous, but were a bit dangerous on the antique pine floors.

"Cassandra, it's not over with the lunch rush. We still have afternoon tea from three until five o'clock today," I reminded her and brushed by with a tray laden with steaming bowls of soup, generous plates of 'Toad in the Hole,' and fresh salads topped with goat cheese, red onions, cranberries and glazed pecans. Lucy's new menu was a big hit with the tourists! I was glad I had worn my practical Clark clogs which hugged my feet with each step I took. If the lunch crowd was any indicator, this was going to be a long day!

"Hey! Where the heck is Sarah anyway?" Olivia asked as she exhaled and blew an auburn tendril of hair out of her eyes. "I'm dying already!"

"She said she had some research to do on the Andrew Jackson Bridge Murders and is at the library looking at microfiche," I answered. "She should be here any minute. I've called her a few times but most likely she has her phone off in the library."

"Amelia, you are needed at the cash register," Cassandra smiled and glided quickly past me. I was so glad that her attorney, Thomas Simpson, had driven into Jonesborough this morning to meet with Lucy. He had helped me when I had found myself on the short list of suspects in the murder of my college roommate and knowing he was handling Lucy's case allowed us to make sure she capitalized on the thousands of people lining the streets of Jonesborough.

National Story Telling Festival had turned the small Main Street of Jonesborough into quite a scene. Massive white tents had popped up all over the town to host the annual event in its fourth decade. Storytelling fans came from as far away as Japan and Australia. The tiny historical town of just over four thousand residents was finding itself host to thousands of visitors who had flocked to hear the tales of such world renowned story tellers as author, playwright and Master Storyteller Kathryn Windham; Appalachian humorist Suzi "Mama" Whaples;

seven time Grammy nominated story teller John McCutcheon; and Native American singer and song writer Bill Miller. It was no wonder Lyla's was hopping today!

"Thank you so much for coming today and I hope you enjoy the rest of your visit to Jonesborough," I smiled and made change for a full and happy patron. Just then the door was thrown open and a cold gust of air blew into the tea room. Guests began visibly shivering with the sudden drop in temperature. A man dressed in navy and red plaid pants and a bright red sweater vest was standing in the doorway, looking about, obviously hoping to make a grand entrance.

"Hello, Sir! Welcome to Lyla's Tea Room," I greeted him enthusiastically. He simply stared through me with a non-chalant expression on his face and said nothing at all. "Will you be joining us for lunch today?" I inquired, not quite sure if he had heard me or not.

"Yes and I require a table in the back corner where I will not be disturbed," he stated rather abruptly. He began turning his head quickly and looking about the tea room almost like a hawk looking for its prey moves its head back and forth in sudden jerky motions.

"I don't seem to have a table in the back available right at the moment. I do, however, have a nice table next to the window over here," I offered and gestured to a vacant table. I had become used to demanding guests running The Pink Dogwood Tea Room over the years and had learned not to get ruffled in too many circumstances.

"No, that table will simply not do. How much longer until the back corner table is available?" he snapped, glancing at his watch impatiently and lifting himself up and down on his toes.

"I'm not sure since they were recently seated. Would you like for me to take your name and reserve that table for you when it becomes available?" It was the best I could offer during Jonesborough's busiest week of the year.

"No, no that will just not do. Might I make a suggestion?" he told me rather than asked me. "I would suggest you offer the couple in the back, the table by the window and allow me my privacy in the back corner," he demanded and adjusted his sweater vest for emphasis. He proudly raised his chin and attempted to look at me down his nose but seemed to be having some difficulty since he was a good two inches shorter than me.

Did I just hear him correctly? Did he tell me to move another table of diners just to accommodate his choice of tables? I had heard it all now! This man was beyond smug and arrogant!

"I'm sorry, Sir, I will not be able to accommodate your request. During National Storytelling Festival, tables are at a premium and though we do our best to please everyone, I would never ask a diner to change tables mid-meal," I calmly told him in a low voice. "I would be happy to offer you the table by the window."

"The name is Frank Dupree and you have just earned Lyla's Tea Room a bad review," he spat and turned quickly on his heel, pushing the door open brusquely and nearly hitting a lady on her way in.

"What was his problem?" Olivia asked as she came up to the hostess area.

"THAT...That was Frank Dupree," I informed her. I could feel my blood pressure spiking a bit at the thought of costing Lyla's Tea Room a bad review. "I cannot believe that grown people act that way! He just said he was going to give Lyla's a bad review," I whispered loudly to Olivia. I was hoping that lunch guests had not witnessed the exchange. Small towns are just full of gossipers!

"Allow me to show you ladies to a table," Olivia jumped right in and seated the startled lady Mr. Dupree had just about hit with the door. "Right this way," she smiled and led them to the window table.

"So, I see you met Frank Dupree," Cassandra walked up and looked out towards the sidewalk. "He's a real piece of work!"

"You were absolutely correct in your analysis of him. I have never met someone who thought he was so important that we should move guests in the midst of their lunch just to accommodate his personal preference for a table!" I was really outraged at his behavior.

"Didn't you know that the whole world revolves around Frank Dupree?" Cassandra said in a mocking tone. "He thought you would recognize him immediately and give him what he wanted."

"I didn't have the foggiest idea of who he was. Just some man in a horrific pair of red and navy plaid pants," I laughed a bit at my own new found streak of meanness.

"You mean you didn't recognize him from all of his cookbooks, his column and the billboards all over town?" Cassandra laughed and sat down to rub her aching feet. "You should have bent over backwards to accommodate 'Emperor Frank!'"

"I hope I haven't cost Lucy a bad write up in *The Dogwood Daily*. That's all she needs right now," I said suddenly worried.

"Don't worry, Amelia," Olivia said approaching our little huddle. "What's he going to say? He couldn't get a table during National Storytelling Festival? Of course he was going to have to wait! It's the busiest weekend of the year!" Olivia reassured me.

"Olivia's right. What harm can he do?" Cassandra agreed.

"He's helped to put a lot of our local restaurants out of business. I'm just glad he liked The Pink Dogwood Tea Room and we ended up getting a good review. I honestly did not recognize him," I told the girls. "I couldn't stand it if I hurt Lucy's business!"

"We better shake a tail feather and get back to the tables," Olivia reminded us. Boy she was a task-master. No wonder why her farm hands were always happy to have a day off! It was difficult for them to keep up the quick pace she had around Riverbend Farm.

"Hi girls," Sarah called out as she came through the door. She was wearing a beige trench coat topped off with a jaunty Irish inspired wool cap. She was beaming ear-to-ear and seemed excited.

"Where the heck have you been all morning? We've been busting our humps here and could have used the extra help," Olivia chastised her. "Get an apron on pronto and help us clear the tables, chop, chop!" she ordered and clapped her hands together twice for emphasis.

"Sorry. I'm so sorry! I just got so caught up with the news articles about The Andrew Jackson Bridge Murders, time got away from me," she said sincerely.

"Not to worry, you're here now," I reassured her. "Come back to the kitchen and tell me what you found out."

"Well, I did find out that the police didn't have many leads since there was very little forensic evidence. The lack of blood, no body was ever found… everything was based on Julie's account and the couple in the car."

"What do you mean 'no body?' He was hit with a car and no body was recovered? Did they check the area hospitals for emergency patients brought in that night?" Olivia reasoned.

"They didn't have any suspects at all?" I asked as Sarah removed her coat and hat and threw an apron over her khaki pants and white button down.

"No body, no injuries, no suspects and to this day, there have been accounts of a man dressed in a black hooded cape seen at the bridge," she said wide-eyed and breathless.

"Here we go again," Olivia said shaking her head, visibly amused. "Another *Sherlock Holmes Masterpiece Classic.* Sarah, you need to spend more time out of the library and in the outdoors! I have no time today for this nonsense again!" Olivia warned as she brought a stack of used plates back to the sanitizing area.

"Okay, Olivia!" Sarah retorted. "If you don't believe in ghosts, I dare you to join me on the Jonesborough Ghost Walk Tour tonight! Dress warm and bring a flashlight…that is if you dare!"

"Oh good gravy, Sarah! This research has got you spooked. There's no such thing as ghosts. And what are we? Five? Are you going to triple dog dare me now?" Olivia was shaking with laughter. "They actually have a tour for *Ghost Busters* like you? Oh, this is hysterical!"

"I'll have you know that Jonesborough is one of the top ten

most haunted towns in the U.S.," Sarah cried. "In fact, the Andrew Jackson Bridge has been featured on 'The Sleuth Masters Club List.'"

"Sleuth Masters? What the heck is that?" Olivia asked, her hands squarely on her hips.

"The Sleuth Masters Club does paranormal research and investigations in the Southeast. You can contact them and they will do an investigation for you," Sarah said shaking her head in the affirmative.

"And let me guess… you're a card carrying member of this Sleuth Masters Club." She washed and dried her hands at the hand washing station in the kitchen before heading back out. She turned around and said over her shoulder, "Okay Sara! I'll take you up on your dare. We'll do the Ghost Walk Tour tonight!"

"She'll change her mind, Amelia! Mark my words," Sarah said and headed out to the dining room to assist with the tables.

"Two trifles and two orders of rum raisin scones, please Darla!" Cassandra called cheerily back to the kitchen. "Amelia, can you help me make a couple pots of tea?"

"Sure. What do you need?"

"I need a pot of assam, a pot of Irish breakfast, a pot of jasmine, and…" she fished in her apron pocket for her order pad. "Oh, yes! A pot of market spice! I love the aroma of that one in particular."

I grabbed four individual two cup porcelain tea pots and began preheating them with hot water. While I filled the T-sacs with two teaspoons of each tea, I turned my attention back to Cassandra and our earlier conversation about Frank Dupree.

"I think Frank Dupree is so self-absorbed and so demanding, I can only imagine how furious he was with Cheryl White when she bought the Parson's Table right from under him. That man has some pent up anger!" I told her as I set a timer for four minutes for each of the teas.

"I told you he has short-man syndrome. And in my book, he's a ticking time-bomb. Let's keep him on the short list of suspects," she laughed at her own joke. "Speaking of suspects, have you heard from your Aunt Imogene today?"

"I've got to call her. Thank you for reminding me. She is supposed to find out more about Delilah Bennett's real estate deal for the Salt House. I'll call her right now. Will you keep an eye on these timers while I give her a quick call?"

"Yes, thanks for making those for me. I'll just run them out to the tables when the timers go off. Gosh, that trifle looks decadent! I'm going to have to get Chef Niles to make that when I get back to Dogwood Cove," she said eyeballing with delight two beautiful hand cut glass bowels filled with layers of lemon sponge cake, raspberries, white billows of cream, and a perfect raspberry with a mint sprig on top.

I found my handbag in the break room and pulled my cell phone out for a quick call to Imogene. She answered on the second ring.

"This is Imogene. How can I make your real estate dreams come true today?"

"Imogene, it's Amelia," I identified myself. "Have you had any luck finding out about Delilah Bennett?" I quietly said into the phone covering my mouth so as not to be overheard by any of the sorority girls helping out in the kitchen.

"Did I ever dig up the dirt," Imogene reported. "I've got a lot to tell you, but I'm on my way to close on a house right now. I'm about to walk out the door."

"Why don't we catch up later tonight? We still have afternoon tea to serve and Sarah has roped Olivia into the Jonesborough Ghost Walk Tour tonight. Do you want to come?" I suggested.

"Well, I haven't been on one of those tours. It sounds like fun. I'll be there. Where should we meet?"

"How about Lyla's at seven o'clock? We can get a quick bite to eat and then head out for the tour. How does that sound?" I suggested.

"Sounds like a plan! I'll see you at seven tonight!" She shrilled and hung up the phone.

Little did I know that there would be more than just ghosts joining us for tonight's tour!

NINE

"When are we meeting Imogene for dinner?" Olivia asked with a lilt in her voice. "I hope it's soon because I am in need of some refueling after today's crowd." She was wearing a warm red barn coat with a brown leather collar, chocolate brown jeans and her Ariat equestrian dark brown ankle high boots. Her hair was pulled back in a loose pony tail at the nape of her neck and showcased a gorgeous pair of amber earrings that were a recent gift from Lincoln.

"I think the four rum raisin scones and two helpings of 'toad in the hole' should hold you over until she gets here," Cassandra teased. She had long since abandoned her Jimmy Choo boots and was dressed more warmly for tonight's events. She had on a black goose down vest with a silver faux fox collar layered over a silver turtleneck, black velvet jeans and comfortable looking black Uga knee high boots. Her large princess cut diamond earrings set in platinum complemented her blonde mane beautifully! There was chic, and then there was Cassandra Reynolds chic!

"Imogene should be here any minute. What are you in the mood for tonight? Italian? Japanese? Mexican?" I asked the group who were becoming restless. "The restaurant next door, Bistro 105, is an intimate little spot and the fried green B.L.T. is one of their most popular dishes!"

"Fried green B.L.T.? I'm sold!" Olivia cheered! She seemed in much better spirits than when we had last talked about Lincoln's marriage proposal. Maybe they had come to some agreement, I hoped.

"Hey everyone!" Sarah waved as she came through the door of Lyla's. She was decked out tonight in a large black parka, blue jeans, black sweatshirt and was toting a hard hat with an enormous hand lamp attached to the front. "Did I miss anything?"

"Well no one will be able to miss you in that get-up!" Olivia remarked sarcastically. "Really Sarah? You look like you are ready to go spelunking with that hard hat. Please tell me you don't plan on wearing that!"

"You would be surprised how many times this hat has come in handy. You'll want to get one," Sarah testified.

"I don't think so, Sarah. Now what have you got in that messenger bag? Rope, candles, a ouija board to communicate with the dead?" Olivia teased.

"Actually, I have with me my EMF meter, a notebook, a video camera, and a compact digital camera."

"What did you just call that gismo? An EMF?" Olivia asked coming over to inspect the contents of Sarah's bag which was now neatly laid out on the table.

"EMF stands for Electromagnetic Field Meter. It has a built in tone to notify you when you are near a ghost or any paranormal activity. I also have an infrared thermometer to measure sudden changes in the temperature.

"Oh, Sarah. You are starting to remind me of Daphne from Scooby Doo. You know, the brainy one?" Olivia declared.

"Is it going to be Bistro 105 tonight then?" I asked hoping

to divert Sarah and Olivia's attention. I was getting worried that the ghost hunting might get in the way of a beautiful friendship.

"Let's do it!" Cassandra affirmed.

"Let me call Imogene and tell her to meet us there. It's just next door from Lyla's." I quickly dialed her number.

"Wow. That's strange! Her phone went straight to voice-mail," I informed the girls.

"Text her or send her a message on Twitter. Then she'll be sure to see it," Olivia suggested.

"Good thinking, Liv! Gosh, I'm not as fast as Imogene on the texting. I rarely do that unless one of the kids needs a quick yes or no. Hold on," I said slowly searching the keypad for the correct letter. "Okay, message sent. I told her to meet up with us at Bistro 105 and then we would head out for the ghost walk tour."

"Good night Darla!" I called back to the kitchen. She was overseeing a young man mopping the floors and finishing some end of the day activities.

"Thanks bunches, Amelia and ladies! Aunt Lucy will be glad to know everything went well today!" she happily called out.

"Get some rest, Darla. Tomorrow is another busy day!" Olivia reminded her.

"I hear you! I will. Thanks!" she replied.

"Boy, I could go for a steak and a glass of wine about now. I'm pooped!" Olivia said as she leaned her head against Cassandra's shoulder for support.

"You and the vino are not a good match!" Cassandra chided.

"For Pete's Sake, Cassandra! It's just *one* glass of wine."

"Remember the bull riding incident at the Lazy Spur after you had a little too much tequila? You dislocated your hip and hobbled around for a month!"

"Anything else, Mother?" Olivia pursed her lips and crossed her arms defiantly. "I don't plan on riding any bulls in Jonesborough on a ghost walk. Are we there yet?"

I pulled open the door to the intimate bistro and stepped up to the hostess stand. It was standing room only tonight with full tables and diners waiting in caloric anticipation.

"Wow! It' a bit more crowded than I thought. Would it be possible to get a table for five?" I asked the young hostess.

"It will be just a few minutes if you don't mind waiting," she replied.

"That will be fine. Thank you!"

"Oh no!" Sarah gasped and placed both of her hands on either side of her face. "It looks like Cheryl's step-daughters are eating dinner with Jake and his parents. He didn't even let me know he was in town," Sarah cried.

"Get a grip, Sarah honey," Cassandra cooed. "Don't you dare let him see that you are upset! Act surprised to see him and aloof. I'll take care of this. You stay here and watch me." She motioned for us to wait and sashayed in the general direction of the White's table. She looked straight ahead, her shoulders back, her confident nature showing in every stride she took across the room. She slowly walked past the White's table and waited for Jake's Mom to notice her.

"Cassandra? Is that you?" Sabrina White called out.

"Oh, my goodness, Sabrina!" Cassandra gushed and effusely hugged Sabrina. "What a small world! What are you doing here?" Cassandra looked over her shoulder at Sarah and winked. The rest of us stood at a safe distance, but due to the restaurant's limited size, were able to see and overhear the conversation.

"Well, you may have heard, Bob's cousin was tragically murdered yesterday. We're here to help the police with the investigation and to make funeral arrangements," Sabrina told her.

Sabrina White was also a mover and shaker in the Dogwood Cove community. She had served on the board of education three consecutive terms and was very involved in various philanthropies about town. She and Cassandra had served together on the board of the ballet. She was a force to be reckoned with and at times I felt that she had kept Sarah and Jake from marrying with her interfering ways.

"Oh, how awful! I'm so sorry for your loss," Cassandra continued. "Bob, my deepest condolences to you and to you too, Jake. I had no idea you were in town."

"Yes, well I wanted to help Mom and Dad with the arrangements and give them support," he explained. "Would you like to have a seat, Cassandra?" Jake offered and stood up to offer his chair.

"Oh, no! That is so kind of you, Jake, but I'm already joining friends for dinner. I'm sorry," she said turning her attention to the two ladies seated to Jake's left. "Where are my manners? We haven't been properly introduced. I'm Cassandra Reynolds," she smiled and extended her hand.

"I'm Barbara Bishop and this is my sister, Irene Bishop," a lady in her mid-thirties with dark brown shoulder length hair introduced herself and politely shook Cassandra's hand.

"Bishop, Bishop! Why does that name sound familiar?" Cassandra asked aloud.

"Barbara and Irene are Dean Bishop's daughters. Their father was married to Cheryl," Sabrina quickly explained.

"Oh, how awful for you!" Cassandra gasped. "I'm so sorry for your loss. You just must be devastated by all this! Bless your hearts!" she cooed shaking her head with sympathy.

Barbara and Irene turned toward each other, both seeming to be at a loss for words. Neither said anything as Cassandra continued.

"When did you two get into town?" she asked, sitting in Jake's vacant chair at the table.

"Oh, we were already in the area attending a real estate convention when we got the news about Cheryl," Irene finally spoke up.

"Oh. You were already in the area? I wasn't aware there was a real estate convention going on," Cassandra commented.

"It is in Gatlinburg this weekend," Irene told her. "We were here enjoying the beautiful fall foliage and seeing the Great Smoky Mountains. We don't have much of a change in seasons down in Florida."

"Well what a coincidence that you were so close! Gatlinburg is just about an hour's drive from here. I'm sure Sabrina and Bob were relieved to have family come at such a terrible time. What a tragedy!" Cassandra continued. "I'm sure it would mean so much to Cheryl that you are here right now. Were you two very close with your step-mother?" Cassandra inquired, doe-eyed and innocent. It's hard not to answer her direct line of questioning, a trait that makes her a formidable opponent in the business world.

"Umm. I'm not sure you would call us a close knit family," Barbara spoke up.

"Oh no? Why not?" Cassandra asked point-blank.

"Let's just say there was a dispute over Daddy's will and real estate holdings," Barbara replied, obviously the take charge dominant sister.

"Oh. A dispute over real estate holdings and a will. I'm sure that put a damper on your relationship!"

Sabrina nearly swallowed her tongue as Cassandra focused her full attention on the ladies. "I actually met your step-mother the day she died. She was a real hum-dinger!"

"Yeah, you could say that!" Barbara piped up and realizing her faux pas, quickly composed herself as she glanced in Sabrina's direction.

"Cassandra, I'm sure your friends are missing you by now," Sabrina suggested.

"Oh, actually we are waiting on a table. So tell me… Barbara. Was Cheryl as ruthless as a step-mother as she was as a business woman?"

"Cassandra! Why I never!" Sabrina blustered.

"Oh, Sabrina, get over it! Everyone knows she used Sarah to get information to purchase real estate in Jonesborough and put Lyla's Tea Room out of business. I'm sure the police have already talked with you about it."

"I don't appreciate the direction of this conversation," Bob spoke up. "You're speaking about my family."

"Daddy. Calm down," Jake said and patted his father's arm. He had not spoken once since Cassandra arrived at their table. He was definitely quiet in the presence of his parents.

"Bob. I mean no offense. We all have family members we are not always so proud of. These girls had quite a history with their step-mother and maybe they could shed some light into who might have held a grudge against Cheryl. Obviously, both of you had something to gain by her demise," Cassandra lobbed a cannon ball across their bows.

"I had nothing to do with her death," Irene said placing her hand against her chest as to suggest she was offended. "I admit I didn't get along with Cheryl and I was furious with Daddy for marrying her, but I would never *KILL* her!"

"Cassandra, I think this conversation has become highly inappropriate," Bob warned her. "I think it would be best if we said good evening and please leave us to our grieving."

"Bob. I'm sorry for your loss. My friend, Lucy Lyle, has been wrongly arrested for Cheryl's murder and I for one will do anything in my power to prove she did not do it. Lucy was a victim of being in the wrong place at the wrong time." She stood up to take her leave, lifting her Louis Vuitton hand bag onto her shoulder.

"Sabrina, Bob, Jake… I'm truly sorry for your loss. Ladies! It was a pleasure," she said and walked away from the group, joining us by the entry way.

"Oh my gosh!" Sarah said. "I can't believe you asked them if they were close to Cheryl!"

"It's best to catch people off-guard. They will rehearse what they will say to the police. To a stranger who asks point-blank, they haven't had time to filter their answer. They tend to be a little more honest.

"So what did you find out? Are they torn up over *Mommy*

Dearest?" Olivia asked sarcastically.

"I'm not sure how they feel about Cheryl, but there is no love loss for you. They are glaring over here, Cassandra," I informed her.

"I'll make it up to Sabrina and Bob later. They were naive about Cheryl and they certainly don't realize they could be sharing a meal with two murderers. Those two were just a stone's throw away in Gatlinburg at a real estate convention. Isn't that a coincidence?" she informed us.

"Has anyone confirmed there was a real estate convention in Gatlinburg? That might be a shady alibi with those two vipers," Olivia surmised.

"Imogene would know. In fact, I'm surprised she hasn't made it here by now. Her closing must have taken much longer than she planned," I thought aloud. I was starting to get a bit worried about her. She wasn't one to miss out on any opportunity to have fun or enjoy a meal with friends. Maybe she had forgotten about our evening plans or didn't get my message.

"Let me check her Twitter account and see if she's been tweeting," Olivia suggested. She put her hand out for my cell phone and went to my address book to look up Aunt Imogene's information. She quickly typed in the appropriate address.

"She hasn't tweeted in over two hours. How weird!" Olivia remarked.

"What was her last tweet?" I asked pulling her hand towards me to see it for myself.

"Meeting the girls for dinner. Big news to share. Lucy Lyle is innocent. Oh, my gosh! She must have discovered something about Delilah Bennett!" I shared with the group. "She must have found out something important. We've got to reach her!"

"Why would she put that on Twitter?" Olivia asked aloud. "Does she want to broadcast to everyone that she knows who did it! She's not very subtle, is she?"

"I've told you that Aunt Imogene doesn't have a filter. She just states whatever is on her mind. She should *NOT* have tweeted about that! I have a feeling she's uncovered something big. I'm going to have to have a talk with her when she gets here about being more careful about what she posts on Twitter," I said with a worried expression on my face.

"You mean *'IF'* she gets here. Where could she be?" Olivia said and spoke aloud the words we were all thinking. Where was Imogene?

TEN

"*L*et's get on with this already!" Olivia said impatiently. "We didn't even have time to order dessert with the long wait for a table. I call Mona Lisa's Gelato on the way back to the hotel!" she cried out like a grade school kid at recess.

"Olivia! Focus on something other than food, okay?" Cassandra scolded. "Poor Amelia is worried sick about Imogene and you are planning your next 'Snack Attack.' Really!" she said huffily.

"Am I really that bad?"

"YES!" We all answered her in unison.

"I'm sorry! It's just my high metabolism. I'll try to keep it to myself. I did pack some trail mix for the tour. Anyone want some?" she asked removing a large ziplock bag from her barn coat.

"No thanks, Olivia, but that was sweet of you to offer," Sarah acknowledged the grand gesture which was not lost on her. Olivia wasn't one to share her food. She was territorial and there never seemed to be enough to go around!

"Where are we meeting the other *Tales From The Crypt* Geeks? She joked as she put a handful of trail mix into her mouth.

"At the Jonesborough Visitor's Center near the entrance to Main Street," Sarah said and led the group down the brick paved sidewalks. "Watch your step," she warned. "A lot of these bricks are uneven and will trip you up."

"I wish the lighting was a bit better. I can hardly see a thing with all the fog. It's creepy!" Olivia whined.

"You're not getting scared of a little fog, are you Olivia?" Cassandra ribbed her playfully. "I'm with you though. It sure is dark out here."

"That's why this hard hat comes in so handy," Sarah said and flipped her head lamp on, like a lone beacon in a snow storm. It actually helped quite a bit.

"Are we almost there? My toes are feeling numb already," I said as I exhaled and saw my own breath. "This tour better be worth venturing out on such a cold night! Anyone have a tissue?"

"I do! Here Amelia," Sarah said and whipped out a pack of tissues from her messenger bag. "Here's the check-in point for the tour. Why don't we go inside and warm up while we are waiting?" she suggested happily.

We quickly paid the cashier for our tickets and took a look around the Jonesborough history museum located inside the Visitor's Center. There were about six other people gathered inside for the tour. The docent was kind enough to offer everyone hot apple cider to warm up our icicle hands.

"If I could have everyone's attention," a young man in an army surplus green jacket addressed the group. "I'm Mike and I will be leading your Jonesborough Ghost Walk Tour of Tennessee's most haunted and historic town tonight. Follow me, *if you dare…*" he laughed dramatically in his best impression of Vincent Price. "If you would like to rent an EMF detector for this tour, Casey will be happy to take care of that for you."

"Olivia. Would you like to rent one?" Sarah asked as she pulled her EMF detector out of her bag. Thankfully, she had switched off her head lamp when we came inside.

"Ahh, I think I'll pass on that," she said as she looked around at the mixed group of college students and adults who were participating in the tour. She leaned closer to me and whispered in my ear, "This group looks like sci-fi convention rejects. Look at all of their EMF gismos." And she was right. The buzz of EMF scanners was filling the air as everyone turned their monitors on. I had to laugh at the bizarre scene in front of us.

"Right this way, everyone," Mike said walking backwards to face our group. "Jonesborough has been said to be one of the ten most haunted places in the United States. That's not surprising since it is Tennessee's oldest town, settled in 1779.

"Our first stop this evening will be at Ruth's Sweet Shoppe, the scene of many malted soda, milkshakes and banana splits. But there seems to be a mischievous ghost who has his own message for the patrons. Walk down the alley just past the building and read the ghostly message from our dearly departed friend," Mike gestured for us to round the corner, lifting his lantern high so that it cast an eerie glow on the side of the building.

"What are we looking for?" Olivia whispered loudly with her hands in her pockets to stay warm. "What's the message?"

We all carefully walked down the alley, Sarah's headlamp leading the way. She turned and faced the bricked side of the building and there it was! The words "Go Away" were visible in bold angry red letters with a drip pattern similar to blood.

"Over the years, previous owners of this building have re-surfaced the brick, even painted it and still these two words always bleed through. And no one seems to know the origins of them. Pretty spooky! Take a few minutes to look around, measure for EMF activity and take pictures. We've seen a lot of paranormal activity in this area."

"I'll tell you the origins of those letters. It's called kids with spray paint," Olivia said bluntly.

"Hush, Olivia! You'll hurt Sarah's feelings," I reminded her. Sarah was walking up and down the alley with her EMF detector and measuring with her infrared thermometer. She was definitely in her element!

"Now if you'll follow me, we will make our way to our next stop…the Stage Coach Inn," Mike said as he led our group up the bricked side walk and across the street. "The Stage Coach Inn is host to one of Jonesborough most famous residents, Davy Crockett."

"I thought Crockett lived in Greeneville," Cassandra piped up.

"Crockett was born not far from here and spent most of his life in East Tennessee. Most likely, you're thinking of Andrew Johnson, the seventeenth President of the United States. There is a National Historic Site in Greeneville where you can visit his homestead and tailor shop. It's worth a trip to the area to explore the cemetery and National Park."

"Thank you, Mike for clearing that up!" Cassandra replied.

"Now remember, ladies and gentlemen. Jonesborough was not the quiet sleepy little town you see before you today. Back in 1821, it was more like the wild West, full of saloons, shootouts, stabbings and frontier chaos. Crockett arrived sometime in 1821 to serve as a member of the U.S. House of Representatives. He was later defeated in the 1834 elections when he took a stand against the Indian Removal Act.

"Jonesborough was still a rough frontier town. That much had not changed," Mike continued. Crockett was often seen carrying his musket and wearing his coon skin cap.

"My kind of man!" Olivia snickered and continued nibbling on her trail mix.

"Many people have reported seeing a young Davy Crockett walking right in front of this door, his musket over his shoulder, his trademark buckskin boots on," Mike concluded.

"Here we go again," Olivia snickered and rolled her eyes.

"I've got a reading," Sarah yelled out. "There's definitely some sort of temperature change right by the front door!"

"Yeah, it's called guests checking in for the night. Watch out Sarah, there's a lady trying to open the front door behind you," Olivia laughed as Sarah nearly bumped into a friendly lady carrying a suit case.

"Olivia, let her enjoy the tour. Try to act a bit frightened every once in a while. It will give her a big thrill," Cassandra quietly pleaded with her best friend.

"I'm just not buying this horse manure about ghosts and ghost writing. This tour just feeds off of people's over-active imaginations. It's for people who watch that ridiculous show *Myth Busters*."

"That may very well be your opinion, but this is for Sarah. Loosen up just a bit and try to have fun," Cassandra concluded.

"If you'll follow me now, we are approaching the Jonesborough Court House where Andrew Jackson practiced law and was the scene of many notorious cases in Washington County.

If you'll walk around the far side of the building, you'll see past the parking lot a covered structure known as the Andrew Jackson Bridge, scene of three grisly murders, most notably one that took place just last night," Mike said and continued walking through the vacant parking lot.

"We won't be able to get any closer because of the crime scene tape, but if you'll look towards the bridge, I'll share with you the unsolved murders of two young lovers, back on a warm summer evening in the late 1940's."

"This will really get Sarah going!" Olivia moaned. Sarah was using her video camera to film zoom shots of the bridge while Mike was talking.

"Julie and Patrick were visiting the local lover's spot when Julie reported a man dressed in black, wielding an axe, came walking across the bridge, over to the couple and fatally hacked poor Patrick. He then turned the axe on Julie who was running across the bridge to escape her caped killer," Mike shared with the captive audience.

"If you look to the left of the bridge, you will notice..."

"Aunt Imogene's car!" Sarah gasped as her video camera zoomed in on a red Lincoln Continental with Imogene's real estate picture on the side.

"What? Where? I asked beginning to run towards the bridge.

"Don't cross the crime scene tape!" Mike yelled after me.

"I don't give a flip about crime scene tape," I yelled back over my shoulder at the stunned tour guide. Wild horses couldn't keep me from Imogene. I tour through the yellow tape as if it were made of tissue paper. My feet flew across the wooden bridge while my heart pounded loudly in my ears.

"Imogene! Imogene! Are you okay?" I screamed as I approached her car, the side door propped open and the engine turned off. I flipped on the interior light and began searching the car, expecting to find her passed out or worse dead.

"Amelia. Is she okay?" Sarah rushed up by my side. "Where is she?" she asked confused, looking around.

"I don't know. Her purse is here. Her keys are in the car. I don't know where she is!" I spoke loudly, panic evident in my voice. I was having trouble thinking straight.

"Sit down Amelia before you pass out," Cassandra suggested. I'm sure she just had a little engine trouble and has gone for help."

"And left her keys and handbag? Not Imogene. Let me check and see if her cell phone is in her handbag." I dug around and quickly located her cell phone. I pulled it out to show everyone. "There is no way she would go anywhere willingly without this," I told them. Mike and the rest of our tour group had caught up to us by this time.

"Is there a problem? Do we need to call for help?" Mike volunteered.

"Yes, call the sheriff and tell him we have a missing person on the Andrew Jackson Bridge," Cassandra barked. "And tell him to get a search team together NOW!"

"Okay! Okay!" Mike shouted excitedly.

"Maybe she got sick while she was driving and pulled over to call for help," Sarah concluded. "Maybe she's at the hospital!"

"I'll call the hospitals," Olivia snapped. "Amelia, press redial and see the last number Imogene dialed. Maybe it's 911."

My hands were shaking as I toured the cell phone key pad and looked for the redial button. I pushed it and as the phone face lit up I was shocked to see that Imogne had been dialing a phone number...my phone number, except the last digit was missing!

ELEVEN

"We've got a search team combing these woods. If she's out there we'll find her. I've got our K-9 unit on the way now," Sheriff Anderson informed me.

"Did someone go by her house and check to see if she's there?" I asked hopefully. "Maybe someone stole her car out of the driveway?" I hopefully suggested

"We sent a patrol car about a half hour ago. She's not home and there's no sign of an incident taking place. I'm afraid this is looking like an abduction," he informed me.

"Sheriff Anderson, I'm Cassandra Reynolds," Cassandra introduced herself and extended her hand. "I would like to offer my helicopter and pilot to assist in an aerial search. My resources are at your disposal."

"Thank you, uh…Mrs. Reynolds. I appreciate the offer. We do have the Washington County Sheriff's helicopters available. The problem is, they are grounded with this thick fog. We'll have to wait until daybreak to get them in the air."

"She'll freeze to death from exposure if we don't find her tonight! We can't wait until the morning to get those helicopters in the air," I reasoned as tears began streaming down my face uncontrollably.

"M'am. We're doing the best we can do with the fog and

the fact that it is night time. I've got ten deputies walking these woods, looking for signs of your Aunt right now. If she's out there, we'll find her." Sheriff Anderson paused as he was called on his radio. "Excuse me, ladies," he said as he turned his back and walked towards his car.

"Daybreak will not be soon enough! We've got to do something. Imogene is pretty spry for someone her age, but I'm worried about the below freezing temperatures this time of year. I sure hope she was dressed in something warm," I said burying my face in Cassandra's shoulder.

"Imogene is a real firecracker. I'm sure she's fine and there's some good explanation for all of this," Cassandra offered and began stroking my head. "They'll find her and she'll be sharing some tall tale, I'm sure."

"Amelia! Have they found Imogene yet?" Shane rushed forward and hugged me hard. "Oh, gosh. I got here as fast as I could!" He held me in a long embrace and buried his face in my hair. "What has the sheriff told you?"

"They are just as confused as we are about what her car was doing abandoned on the bridge. Shane, she left the keys in the car, her purse *and* her cell phone. Imogene doesn't go anywhere without her cell phone!"

"Why don't we get you inside somewhere warm and I will talk with the sheriff. There's nothing you can accomplish standing out here freezing!" Shane said. "Cassandra, are any of the shops or restaurants still open? Maybe you can take Amelia for a cup of coffee and have everybody warm up. It looks like this may be a long night."

"Darla may still be at Lyla's. They were still cleaning up

when we left. Maybe a strong pot of tea would do us all some good and help us focus on what we can do," Cassandra agreed. "Come on Amelia, let's get you inside," she said and rubbed my arms to help warm me up.

"Shane, call my cell phone the minute you hear anything, O.K?"

"I will. Don't worry!" he said and strode over to the Sheriff's vehicle.

"Was that Shane?" Olivia asked joining us.

"Yeah, he just got here. He's going to talk with the Sheriff and keep us updated," I quickly told her.

"We're headed over to Lyla's to get some hot tea and warm up. Are you coming?" Cassandra asked.

"Yeah. Let me go grab Sarah. She's got her EMF counter out looking for the Andrew Jackson Bridge Murderer. I worry about that girl," she said shaking her head and going in Sarah's direction.

We were lucky that Darla was still at the tea room going over the books. The lights were on and we rapped on the window to get her attention.

"Hey, you just couldn't stay away!" she joked. "Should I get your aprons out and get some extra help in the kitchen?" she smiled as she opened the door, quite oblivious to the cause of the ongoing activity.

"Would you mind if we came in to warm up and have a pot of tea?" Cassandra requested. "We may be up for a while tonight."

"Sure! Of course!" she said gesturing for us to come in. "What's going on down there anyway? Has someone been in an accident? I saw the blue lights flashing."

"It's Imogene…she's missing and they fond her car abandoned on the Andrew Jackson Bridge," Cassandra informed her.

"Oh, no! Amelia, I'm so sorry!" Darla cried. "What happened?"

"We don't know what has happened to her. The Sheriff thinks it's a possible abduction," I said and slid behind a table. I sat down heavily feeling the weight of the evening close upon me.

"Abduction? Why would someone want to kidnap her? That doesn't make any sense!" Darla stated.

"Well, it makes sense if Imogene snooped around and found something out this afternoon. The last time I spoke with her, she had something important to tell me about Delilah Bennet."

"I'll start some hot water for tea and coffee for the deputies. You stay put!" Darla ordered and hurried back to the kitchen.

"How do you know Imogene talked with Delilah Bennett?" Cassandra asked me patting my hands. "Are you getting warm yet?"

"Imogene said something about big news to tell me. She said she had dug up some dirt on Delilah and was looking into some real estate transactions."

"Should we tell the Sheriff about Delilah?" Cassandra suggested. "I think it could be important for him to know, don't you?"

"Yeah. I didn't even think about that. I just am so worried about her! What has she gotten herself into?"

"If I know Imogene, she's just fine!" Olivia said encouragingly and pulled up a chair. "She's probably giving someone heck even now as we speak!"

"Where's Sarah?" Cassandra asked turning around and looking in the direction of the door. "Didn't you tell her we were walking over here?"

"I told her. She said she wanted to do a little research of her own. I didn't ask what she meant," Olivia stated.

"Here is a pot of lapsang souchong tea. This will definitely keep you up tonight," Darla cautioned.

"Thanks Darla," I said and pulled out a chair for her. "Would you like to sit down?"

"I thought I would take some coffee and muffins out to the deputies. They are going to need some caffeine to get through tonight. I'll be right back."

"You're a real sweet heart. You're Aunt Lucy must be so proud of you for running Lyla's so well in her absence."

"Thank you, Mrs. Reynolds. I love working here. I have a real passion for food. I hope when Aunt Lucy comes back, she'll have me stay on full time."

"She'd be a fool not to have you stay on. She needs someone she can trust to help her run things. I'm sure we'll be seeing much more of you at Lyla's from now on," I reassured her.

"Thanks. I'll be just a minute."

"Whoa! Smell that tea. Doesn't it smell like a camp fire?" Olivia asked and watched our expressions as we both inhaled its heady aroma.

"Lapsang souchong is roasted in long strips over cypress fires. That's why it reminds you of a camp fire," I informed her.

"Well if it is as strong as it smells, I shouldn't have a problem staying up all night," Cassandra commented.

We slowly savored our tea, letting the hot liquid coat our

throats and gradually warm our bodies. It felt good to hold the warm tea cup and just be still for a moment.

"I want to help find Imogene," Olivia said after a few minutes of silence. "I think I may know of a way to do it."

"How?" Cassandra asked her.

"I thought maybe I could ask some of my horseback riding friends to help ride and comb these woods. They are so thick, it would be much easier to get through on horseback," she suggested.

"Olivia Rivers! That's probably the best idea I've heard all night," Cassandra jumped up from her chair and rushed over to kiss Olivia on top of the head.

"Let's not get carried away, Cassandra. It's still going to be hard to maneuver in such a mountainous area."

"Yeah, but easier than walking through the brush and you'll have the advantage of eyes up a little higher," Cassandra added.

"Thank you, Olivia. Imogene will be glad to know you are helping to look for her," I told her. "Thank you both for just being here."

"I wish there was something more we could do," Cassandra spoke out loud.

"Cassandra, you came here to help Lucy out with her business, you've helped by having Reynolds's top attorney represent Lucy when she was arrested, and you helped work in the tea room today during National Storytelling Festival… I think you have done so much already!" I listed off to her.

"I just wish there was something more I could do," she whined. "I'm not used to sitting on the sidelines and watching as a spectator."

"Well, maybe you and I should have a talk with Delilah Bennet first thing in the morning. Maybe she will tell us what they talked about," I said rather hopefully.

"That's a good idea. I'm going to make a few phone calls tonight to mobilize my four legged friends," Olivia said and pulled out her cell phone. I also am going to have Dan load the horse trailer from Riverbend Ranch and get my farm hands to join the search."

"Oh, thank you, Olivia!" I said and hugged her fiercely. "I hope they find her tonight, but just in case they don't, it's good to know that I have friends willing to help."

Just then Shane came through the door and joined us at our table. His face had a very grave expression.

"Anything yet?" I asked him.

He plopped down in a chair and ran his fingers through his hair.

"Nothing yet. Don't worry, Amelia. They will find her. I think Sheriff Anderson used to be one of your Aunt's beaus back in the day. He seems to have a vested interest in finding her," he sheepishly smiled.

"Aunt Imogene and Sheriff Anderson? I didn't know anything about that!" I told him.

"Your Aunt Imogene was a wild girl back in the day. I can imagine!" Olivia laughed. "It sounds as if she had many boyfriends."

We all laughed thinking of Aunt Imogene in her prime, sneaking off to the Andrew Jackson Bridge even though her Daddy would have skinned her alive!

"Do you think it's possible that Imogene was looking

around the bridge for a clue?" I suddenly asked sitting up a bit straighter. "Maybe she remembered something from her past about the bridge?"

"That would make sense as to why her car was left on the bridge," Cassandra agreed. "What could she have been looking for, I wonder?"

"What if Sarah's right and this has something to do with the Andrew Jackson Bridge Murderer?" Olivia offered.

"You mean the old murders from the 1940's?" Shane asked. "What does that have to do with Imogene's disappearance?"

"We think Cheryl White's death was made to look like the Andrew Jackson Bridge Murders," I told him. "A witness saw a black figure in a hooded cape. Sarah's been doing some research on the ghost stories from the area," I informed him.

"And most likely freaking everyone out!" Shane said. "What does a murder from over 70 years ago have to do with Cheryl White?"

"Maybe nothing at all, but Imogene was exploring some alternative motives. She was going to meet tonight and tell me about her conversation with Delilah Bennet and some dirt she had found out about her."

"Delilah Bennet? I don't get it? What am I missing?" Shane asked confused.

"Delilah was in the process of buying the Salt House when Cheryl swooped in and closed the deal. Delilah was apparently quite angry about it," Olivia told him.

"And then don't forget the lovely Bishop girls," Cassandra added. "I still think their little story about being in the area for a real estate convention sounds fishy. They had more to gain than anyone from Cheryl's death."

"Bishop girls?" Shane asked.

"Cheryl's step-daughters. They were contesting their father's will," I quickly filled him in.

"And they were here? Why?" he asked.

"They were playing the dutiful role of grieving family members in front of Sabrina and Bob White," Olivia told him. "They sure had Sabrina snowed with their innocent act. I wouldn't be surprised if she ran them out of town when Cassandra told her the truth about their relationship with 'Cruella DeVille!'"

"Sabrina and Bob White are here too?" he asked dumbfounded. "I have missed out on everything and how long has it been since you left Dogwood Cove? A little over twenty-four hours?" he said amazed.

"Hey. Take it easy, Shane!" Olivia ribbed him. "We were just here to help a friend. We didn't ask for all this!"

"All I'm saying is that it just seems like whenever you four get together, trouble follows!" He stirred sugar into his tea and took a long sip. "Good tea. Must be from the Fujain Province.

"You tea people," Olivia smirked. "We can be in the middle of a crisis, and you'll stop to comment on how lovely the tea is," she teased and stuck out her pinky.

"You know who could really help right now?" Cassandra said changing the subject. "Lincoln!"

"Lincoln? How is the old guy?" Shane asked Olivia.

"Bad idea, Cassandra," Olivia shook her head adamantly.

"Why? If anyone knows how to help the police or organize a search, it's Lincoln!" Shane continued oblivious to Olivia's uncomfortable mood.

"Cassandra, zip your lip!" Olivia warned.

"I will do no such thing," Cassandra shot back.

"Hey, what's going on with Lincoln?" Shane asked.

"Nothing! Nothing at all!" Olivia glared at Cassandra. "We are just taking a little break for now."

"What? Oh, no! Olivia! What did you do?" Shane asked turning towards her. "He's such a great guy!"

"Why does everyone always think it's my fault?" Olivia hissed. "As if he has to tolerate so much dating me. 'Olivia... What did you do?'" she mocked Shane. "Could it be, just for once, that I didn't do anything at all!"

"I'm sorry, Liv. I shouldn't have jumped to conclusions. It's just that sometimes...sometimes..." he trailed off.

"Sometimes what?" Olivia demanded placing her tea cup down on her saucer. "Go ahead Shane and get it out. Sometimes what?" she demanded.

"Sometimes, you can be a bit intimidating to some of the men you date," he finished.

"I don't think you intimidate Lincoln. I think you guys are a great couple!"

"Yeah, well maybe you wouldn't think so if you really knew him like I do," Olivia continued, visibly angry and frustrated. "Why does everyone take his side?"

"Olivia honey," Cassandra said in a calming tone, "We just want you to be happy!"

"Well moving to Dallas isn't going to make me happy!" Olivia said defensively.

"He wants you to move to Dallas?" Shane butted in.

"He wants to marry her," Cassandra explained.

"That's great!" Shane said enthusiastically. I shook my head no as he looked at me quizzically.

"Shane, he wants Olivia to marry him and move to Dallas. She has Riverbend Farm and all the kids to think about," I explained to him.

"Yeah. That would be a tough decision. I'm sorry, Liv. I had no idea. I still think he's a great guy! I hope you can work it out!" he said.

"I don't see how. I'm just not meant to fall in love and have a relationship with anyone. It's not in the cards for me like for you and Amelia and Cassandra and Doug," she complained.

"Liv, I think you and Lincoln can work this out. Call him!" Cassandra urged her.

"He said we should take a break and that's what I'm giving him. Don't you interfere!" she warned Cassandra.

"By doing what?" Cassandra snapped.

"By calling him. Stay out of it, Cassandra!"

"I will. I will, okay! Gosh!" she said defensively.

"Hey! Shane said suddenly. "Where's the fourth Musketeer? I last saw Sarah with a some kind of helmet rigged up with a headlamp poking around the bridge."

"*The Pink Panther* strikes again!" Olivia laughed. "That girl cracks me up with her naïve ways. She really believes in the Andrew Jackson Bridge ghost. She's probably holding a séance and calling on the ghost of that librarian to help her."

"Olivia, you can be so mean," Cassandra told her. "It's Sarah's naïveté that makes her so special. She loves with all her heart and she's such a good friend to all of us."

"I wasn't trying to say anything bad about Sarah, I just

think she's too gullible and it will end up hurting her," Olivia explained.

"Speaking of Sarah, I felt terrible about Jake not calling her and letting her know he was in town today," I reminded them. "I'm starting to think maybe she deserves someone better than Jake."

"I agree. He just sat there and let his mother do all the talking. It's like he can't think for himself," Olivia agreed. "Lincoln wouldn't put up with that for a minute."

"Precisely!" Cassandra grinned from ear-to-ear.

"Okay. I'm going to head back out," Shane said knowing when to take his lead. "Amelia, honey, try not to worry! I'll keep you posted," he said and kissed me sweetly on the lips.

"I'll be out in a few minutes," I called after him.

"I'm going to make a few phone calls and get some supplies together for the riders," Olivia informed us. "Any idea what might be open this late?"

"What do you need?" I asked.

"Flashlights, protein bars for the riders, water bottles, blankets, gloves," Olivia listed.

"There's a twenty-four hour Walmart and Home Depot open just a short drive on highway 11 E towards Johnson City. They should have everything you need. Want some company?" Cassandra volunteered.

"That would be great. Yeah. Come with me," Olivia agreed.

"I'm going back out to check on Sarah and get an update from the Sheriff. I think I will also keep the coffee and muffins going for the search team. It will give me something to do." I volunteered.

"Okay. Let's meet back in about an hour and a half," Olivia said glancing down at her watch. "Cassandra and I will pick up some breakfast biscuits for everyone. You don't need to worry about anything right now, Amelia."

"Thank you both. Hopefully we'll have some news before daybreak," I added.

There would definitely be some news, but not what I was hoping. Daybreak would reveal many clues.

TWELVE

"We will have the helicopters airborne as soon as this fog burns off," Sheriff Anderson quickly updated me. "The K-9 handlers are still out there and hopefully we will get a good lead," he concluded.

"Sheriff, my Aunt was helping to clear her good friend, Lucy Lyle. She was looking into some real estate deals involving Cheryl White and Delilah Bennet."

"I wasn't aware of any connection between the two of them," Sheriff Anderson said and took another sip of his steaming hot coffee. "What exactly did she tell you?"

"The last conversation I had on the phone with Imogene was that she had dug up some dirt on Delilah Bennet and it had something to do with the Salt House. She was meeting me for dinner at seven o'clock and said she would tell me what she found out. That was the last time I spoke to her," I explained.

"Your Aunt should have been more careful with what and who she was getting involved with. We've had a bit of trouble in the past with the Bennet's and that whole gas price fixing scheme. I think it would be best for a deputy to pick up Mrs. Bennet for questioning." He gestured to one of his deputies nearby. "Deputy Williams, please bring Delilah Bennet to the station for questioning in regards to the disappearance of Imogene Smith."

"Right away, Sheriff," Deputy Williams replied.

"I will have Detective Deakins handle this matter personally," he assured me. "Let your red headed friend know that I would like to meet with the volunteers before they ride off. I want to make sure they have constant radio communication and also for them to realize how dangerous this mission is. The last thing we need is to have another person become hurt or need to be rescued today."

"Yes, Sheriff. I will let Olivia know."

"We'll find her, Mrs. Spencer. Your Aunt Imogene is a fine lady. I will do everything in my power to return her to your family unharmed," he stated looking me square in the eyes with determination.

"Thank you, Sheriff," I smiled and patted his arm. Imogene would be glad to know so many people were helping to find her.

Olivia's ranch foreman, Dan, arrived with the six stall horse trailer and several farm hands. The impressive trailer had a tack area, sleeping quarters and about every necessity one would need when traveling with an equine. It was certainly good to see some familiar Dogwood Cove faces this early morning.

"Hey Dan! Thanks for coming so quickly!" I waved as he lowered the window. Just pull in behind the court house," I pointed to the back parking lot area. "Olivia has some other riders gathering back there," I gestured.

"I'm sorry to hear about your aunt, Amelia. Don't you worry. We'll find her!" he said and moved the truck and trailer towards the rear of the court house. The farm heads nodded respectfully as they drove by.

"Where have you been?" I asked Shane as he approached me from the opposite end of the parking lot.

"Oh, running an errand of my own," he smiled mischievously.

"Shane Spencer. What have you been up to?"

"Nothing. Nothing. What did the Sheriff say?" he asked changing the subject.

"He wants to meet with the volunteer riders before they head out and go over some things with them. He's concerned about their safety." I put my hands in my back pockets and looked quizzically at Shane.

"What errand were you running? I didn't see you leave," I continued to question him.

"I plead the fifth! Hey, I'm going to see if Olivia has an extra horse. Maybe I can ride with the group."

"Be sure to eat something before you leave," I nagged him. Cassandra walked towards me wearing an orange wool poncho over brown wool pants. She had on chocolate brown leather gloves and matching boots.

"Speaking of eating, I think you need to eat breakfast," she reminded me.

"I'm fine. I'm fine. Food is the last thing on my mind right now," I told her.

"You've got to keep up your strength and it probably would be a good idea for you to come back to the hotel and get a short nap, don't you think?" Cassandra recommended.

"I wouldn't be able to sleep, but thank you!" I said grabbing her hand to squeeze it.

"At least take a shower and change your clothes. It may be a long day."

"A hot shower sounds wonderful right now. Maybe then I could warm up the tips of my toes which feel like they are probably purple by now. Let me tell Shane where I'm going and see Olivia and the other volunteers off first."

We walked towards the back of the court house parking lot which was now filled with dozens of volunteers and their four legged companions. There were at least a dozen horse trailers lined up and Olivia was passing biscuits out to each of the riders. A white tent from the National Story Telling Festival was now serving as a makeshift headquarters for the sheriff's command center. Sheriff Anderson was meeting with the riders and showing them coordinates on a map he had copied for each of them.

"This area marked in red to the northwest is Devil's Falls. I would like to remind you that part of that trail is washed out, so I don't want any of you taking any chances getting stranded or hurt that way. The last thing we want is for this to become a search and rescue mission for our rescuers," he lectured.

"Now, I've equipped each team of two riders with a radio. That way we can keep in contact at all times. If you should see anyone or anything suspicious, do not approach! I repeat! DO NOT APPROACH. Call for help and make sure you radio your coordinates. I don't want any Wyatt Earp's in this outfit. We have a strict protocol we follow in these situations.

"We've already got two choppers in the air searching. We will do our best not to get too close to you riders and spook your horses. Are there any questions?" he addressed the group.

"What if we should come across a crime scene?" one rider asked uncomfortably.

"Good question. Do your best not to disturb the area. Radio us with your coordinates and we will secure the area. It's best to leave everything as undisturbed as possible," he directed. "Any other questions?" he paused. "Please stay with your designated partners and keep your radio frequencies on channel 112. Thank you for your time today! Be safe and let's ride out!"

"Olivia!" I called out. "Keep an eye on Shane for me. It's been a while since he's ridden."

"Will do. Don't worry, Amelia. We'll find Imogene and bring her back safe and sound!" she reassured me.

"I'll have my cell phone with me at all times," I told her. "I'm just going to run to the hotel and change clothes."

"Okay. I'll see you shortly and hopefully with some good news." She turned her quarter horse, Maggie May, around and rode to the front of the line. Maggie May was much like her owner, not one to be left behind. She was the Alpha female at Riverbend Farms.

"Let's ride out!" Olivia called to the dozens of riders. Shane waved goodbye and headed into the dense forest behind historic Jonesborough. Though the fog was burning off, it still looked a bit sinister.

"I hope they'll be okay," I told Cassandra. "I hope they find her soon."

We walked back through the parking lot and watched as the streets of Jonesborough began to fill for the day's festivities. Somehow, it just didn't seem right. Everyone was bustling about as if nothing happened, but my world had stopped and come crashing down. The only reminder of what had happened was another display of yellow crime scene tape across the bridge and around the area where Imogene's car still remained. Detectives were on the scene photographing the interior, dusting the door handles and dashboard and collecting various samples in brown paper bags.

"This looks like a bad rendition of C.S.I." I said to Cassandra as we walked back towards Lyla's. "I can't believe this is happening!"

"Don't look at that, Amelia. Let's head over to my car. I parked right here in front of Lyla's," she said as she walked across the street.

"So you're the little trouble maker who sent the Sheriff over to my home at the crack of dawn this morning," a man in bib overalls and combat boots addressed us as he walked towards us.

"Excuse me?" Cassandra addressed the hostile stranger. "Who are you?"

"The name is Bennett. Doak Bennett. And you would be?" he asked hooking his thumbs behind his bib straps.

"Cassandra Reynolds. Mr. Bennett. What seems to be the problem?" She asked in a very authoritative manner.

"Cassandra Reynolds as in Reynolds's Chocolate Company? Oh, so we hang with the big boys," he gestured to me by nodding his head and spat a large plug of tobacco out on the sidewalk. I stepped back to avoid my shoes getting splattered.

"If you'll excuse us, Mr. Bennett." Cassandra continued walking towards the car.

"Any questions that detective has about your Aunt, he may as well be askin' me since I was there when she came by shootin' Delilah so many questions about that Cheryl White woman and the Salt House."

We stopped midstride and turned to look at Mr. Bennett.

What did he know that he would be willing to share with us?

"You saw my Aunt Imogene?" I asked him straightening my back to show him I wasn't intimidated by him. "What did you do to her?" I demanded.

"I didn't do nothin' to your aunt. She's the one that comes a ridin' up in her fancy red car asking about what happened with our bid on the Salt House. We had a nice little talk and she and Delilah got reacquainted, just like old times."

"Just like old times?" I asked Mr. Bennett.

"Yeah. We all went to high school together. I've known Imogene for years. She's a fine lady."

So far the Bennetts seemed harmless. I was hoping that maybe he could shed some light as to where Imogene was headed when she left his home.

"So what did Imogene ask about?"

"She wanted to know why our financing fell through at the last minute. I still can't figure that out to this day. We were all set to sign the paperwork at the bank when I got a call from the bank President saying that there was a last minute delay from the mortgage company and it would be another week before he could have the paper work together. That was just enough time for that woman to swoop in and seal the deal," he complained.

"Delilah had her heart on that place. She wanted to showcase her grandmother's quilts, teach quilting classes and sell antiques. It would have been perfect for her," he said kicking a rock with his toe. "I know the delay from the bank was because of the accusations about gas price fixing."

"Can you prove that?" Cassandra asked.

"Well, Delilah does some transcriptions up at the courthouse and she'd come across some legal papers recently regarding Cheryl White's real estate holdings. Someone was giving her tax exemptions on her property. I've never before in my life seen anythin' like it!" Bennett said shaking his head perplexed. "That woman was an outsider and got more favors than any case of nepotism I have ever heard of," he concluded scratching his head as if perplexed.

"Why would anyone do Cheryl favors?" I asked Cassandra. "She was a newcomer to the area by all accounts and hardly knew anyone."

"Did Imogene say anything to you about what she thought?" I asked Mr. Bennett.

"She said she had someone to go see and took off. That was the last time I saw her. I sure do feel terrible about your aunt. I hope they find her soon."

"Thank you, Mr. Bennett. And thank Mrs. Bennett for talking with the Sheriff. I'm sure they will find her soon."

"Let's get you back to the hotel, Amelia," Cassandra said guiding me with my elbow.

"First, let's get Sarah. She must be at Lyla's," I remembered.

I opened the door and walked in as Darla was just getting ready to serve coffee and tea to the morning storytelling tourists.

"Any news yet?" She asked hopefully.

"No, we just swung by to see if Sarah wanted to come back to the hotel to shower and change," I told her.

"I haven't seen her since you left for dinner last night," Darla remarked.

"What? She didn't come in out of the cold and at least get a cup of tea?" Cassandra asked amazed. "Do you think she went out with the rescue group?"

"I didn't see her this morning with the volunteers. In fact, I haven't heard any mention of her since Shane arrived and said he saw her around the bridge with her head lamp lit. Oh, no, Cassandra! Do you think something has happened to her?" I asked, panic rising in my voice.

"Let's go back to the volunteer tent and see if we can find her. If not, we better let Sheriff Anderson know."

Where was Sarah and what trouble had she gotten herself into?

THIRTEEN

"Sheriff Anderson, I believe one of our search party has also gone missing," I informed him under the make-shift headquarters."

"Who has gone missing?" he suddenly looked up from his computer and grabbed his radio.

"Sarah. Sarah McCaffrey. My friend from Dogwood Cove. She was last seen around the base of the bridge."

"The little gal dressed in the black parka with the head-lamp?" he asked.

"Yeah. The little gal with the headlamp," Cassandra added.

"When was she last seen?" he said.

"It was sometime around eleven o'clock when Shane arrived. He saw her searching around the base of the bridge."

Sheriff Anderson grabbed a K-9 deputy and raced towards the bridge. "Collins! Follow me!"

"What should we do Cassandra?"

"I say let's follow them," she said and grabbed my arm. We started running after Deputy Collins and the formidable looking German Shepard police dog.

Sheriff Anderson was already at the base of the bridge examining the area for clues as to Sarah's disappearance.

"What's this? He asked as he picked up a foreign object

with his gloved hand.

"Oh, my gosh! It's Sarah's infrared thermometer. She must have been taking measurements down here.

"We've got something else, Sheriff Anderson!" Deputy Collins called leaning over something on the ground.

"Looks like a glove," Sheriff Anderson said. "Could this belong to Ms. McCaffrey?" he asked looking up at me.

"She was wearing black knit gloves," I said.

"These are black knit, Collins. Let's see if the dog can pick up her scent," he commanded.

Deputy Collins held the glove up to the dog's snout and began giving him commands.

"Cassandra! Why would Sarah's infrared thermometer and her glove be on the ground?"

"Maybe she was leaving a trail for us to follow?" she suggested. "Maybe she got the feeling she found a lead and something might happen to her. I don't know!" We were both hanging on to each other for support.

The K-9 dog began excitedly barking and began sniffing around the support posts. He went a foot or so and changed direction. The dog moved over to a grassy area and began following the river. The police dog came to a large bush under the wooden infrastructure and began barking wildly.

"What is it boy?" Deputy Collins asked patting the dog. The dog continued barking incessantly.

"Sheriff Anderson. There's got to be something here," Deputy Collins shouted.

"Let me see," Anderson moved forward and began parting the bush to try to see what was agitating the dog. "We've got something behind this bush." He whipped his flashlight out and switched it on. "Collins. Get over here!"

"Oh no, Cassandra! They've found Sarah!" I started crying.

Sheriff Anderson radioed for back up. "We need a couple of deputies under the Andrew Jackson Bridge. We've found an opening leading underground. Get a search party down here immediately," he barked into his radio. "And bring some search lights."

"An opening? Oh, thank goodness!" Cassandra caught her breath. "She's okay."

Six deputies scurried down the river bank rushing forward to join their leader.

"Ladies, I'm afraid I need to ask you to return to the tent area. This could possibly become dangerous. I will keep in close contact and let you know just as soon as we do about your Aunt and Miss McCaffrey," he apologized.

"We'll wait in the tent," Cassandra nodded and turned around to head back toward higher ground.

We looked back to see Sheriff Anderson and his men enter the opening, guns drawn.

"Oh, Amelia! What have they gotten themselves into?"

"I wish he would let us go in there with them," I complained.

"And do what? Risk getting in the middle of a cross-fire? We don't know who or what we're dealing with, remember? All we know is that someone killed Cheryl and there is a murderer still on the loose," she reminded me.

We quickly approached the tented area of the parking lot, hoping the deputies monitoring the radio and computer had some sort of news.

"Amelia, Cassandra, I got here as fast as I could," Dallas Detective Matt Lincoln said and hugged both of us.

"Lincoln, when did you get here?" I asked in total surprise.

"Shane called last night when Imogene went missing and I caught a direct flight from DFW to the tri-cities airport this morning. I just was getting updated by the deputies here. It sounds like they have a lead."

"Yes. It's some kind of opening under the bridge," Cassandra informed him. "They were just going in, pistols drawn when we left."

"Well, the best thing we can do now is wait for some news from the Sheriff. Waiting is always the hardest part," Lincoln said and looked off into the distance. I couldn't help but wonder if he was referring to the investigation or Olivia.

"Hey, does Olivia know you are here?" Cassandra asked lightly slapping him in the arm to get his attention.

"No. I didn't tell her. She has no idea. I think she might be upset if she knew."

"Lincoln, I'm not one to pry, but in this case, I'm going to do just that," Cassandra warned him. "You and Olivia are both like a couple of love sick school kids. You are good together! You belong together. Whatever obstacles you are facing, you can work it out!" she encouraged him.

"That's what I've told her. I've never met anyone like Olivia. She's my little spitfire and I'm madly in love with her. I intend to tell her that just as soon as I see her… that is if she'll still have me," he trailed off looking dejected and forlorn.

Was this the same Matt Lincoln who had interrogated me like I was a notorious criminal? I couldn't believe how different he seemed. Olivia had definitely affected him.

"Lincoln, she will be so happy to see you! She's been miserable ever since you two decided to take a break," I told him.

"Take a break? Is that what she told you?" he asked sounding amazed. "She told me she didn't want me making a sacrifice and moving to Dogwood Cove just for her. She wanted me to stay on the force in Dallas and forget all about her."

"What?" Cassandra gasped. "That's not what she told us!"

"Well, while I'm out here, I'll be interviewing for a position with the Dogwood Cove police department. I'm officially going to become a Tennessee Hillbilly!" Lincoln joked.

"Oh, Matt! How wonderful! Now Olivia will not have to move to Dallas!" Cassandra jumped up and down with glee. "Let me throw the wedding at my lake house. Doug and I insist on doing that for you!"

"That's kind of you, Cassandra. Very kind, but first I must make it official and ask my little firecracker for her hand in marriage." He reached into his pocket and pulled out a beautiful emerald ring encircled with diamonds. The setting was just perfect!

"Do you think she'll like it?" he asked hopefully.

"Do I think she'll like it? I think she'll love it!" Cassandra gushed and kissed Lincoln on the cheek. "Oh, I just knew when I saw the sparks fly between the two of you at the police station that you were 'The One!' " Cassandra cried.

"Well that sounds like a strange beginning, but appropriate in my line of work. I was worried the ring might be too flashy for Olivia's taste," he continued truly concerned.

"There's no such thing as too flashy or too much in my

book. She'll love it! I'm training her to up her wardrobe and accessories anyway. This ring is perfect for her. Good choice!" Cassandra said as her eyes filled with tears and she reached into her hand bag for a tissue.

"Now if we could just get Sarah into a happier relationship," I nodded in the direction of Jake White, standing near the tent with a group of media representatives. Satellite camera trucks and reporters were conducting live interviews, holding their ear pieces to hear above the noisy festival activities.

"The Sheriff has asked for an EMS team to meet them under the bridge," a deputy informed Lincoln.

"Oh, no!" I said and turned to run back to the bridge.

"Amelia, stay here. I'll go!" Lincoln shouted and took off towards the river bank.

"Oh, Cassandra. We get good news one minute and bad the next. Please let everyone be okay!"

"They will be honey, they will be!" she said reassuring herself as much as me.

"Mrs. Spencer, they are calling for you to come down," a female deputy relayed the request.

"Are they okay? Has anyone been hurt?" I asked her.

"I'm sorry M'am. I don't know anything yet," she smiled hopefully at me.

"Come on, Cassandra. Let's get down there," I said as we held hands and ran together. *Why hadn't I joined cross country team in high school?* I thought to myself.

Lincoln was standing in front of a gurney, his large frame blocking my view. Just then I saw Imogene's long red fingernails playfully smack Lincoln's arm. Oh thank goodness!

"Aunt Imogene! Are you okay? You gave us quite a fright!" I scolded her as I quickly enveloped her in a tight hug. "You look terrible!"

"I'm fine. Just need to freshen up the lipstick and get warmed up! I have told these nice ambulance personnel that I do not need to go to the hospital. What I need is a stiff brandy and a hot soaking bubble bath!"

"Aunt Imogene, I would feel so much better if you did let them check you out at the hospital. You had to be freezing last night. What happened anyway?"

"You can read all about it on my twitter. I plan on updating everyone at the same time so I don't have to keep telling the same story over and over again. Let's just say that it involves sex tapes, a town council member and a lost underground tunnel."

"Sex tapes? I don't even want to know! What town council member?"

"Speaking of tunnels, have you seen Sarah?" Cassandra asked with a scared expression.

"Oh, thank goodness for Sarah! That girl is a smart cookie. If it weren't for her, I don't think anyone would have found me in time!" Imogene declared as the EMS team lifted her up into the waiting ambulance. "I'll see you later," Imogene waved as they closed the doors.

I ran to the ambulance door and opened it. "I will be at the hospital as soon as I can," I told her.

"No worries, Amelia. I'm sure they'll keep me there for hours. Come when you can. Ta ta for now!" she cried happily.

"Where's Sarah?" Cassandra asked a deputy coming from the opening under the bridge.

"She's on her way out," he told us.

"Oh, Sarah!" Cassandra shouted as we ran towards our long lost friend. Deputy Collins and his German Shepard were leading her out. Her headlamp was glowing and she held onto her hard hat as she gave each of us a big hug.

"Oh, do I ever have so much to tell you!" Sarah said excitedly.

"Miss McCaffrey," Deputy Collins interrupted. "I'm glad to know you are okay."

"Oh, how can I ever thank you," Sarah said looking up at him with adoration written all over her face. "You saved my life!"

"It was nothing, M'am," he politely said and tipped his hat respectfully. "If it weren't for the trail of clues you left, we may very well be investigating another murder."

"Sarah, Sarah!" Jake White yelled as he scurried down the river bank. "Are you all right? When I heard you were missing, I didn't know what to do!"

"I'm fine, Jake. You might want to interview Deputy Collins, over here. He just saved my life," Sarah added and smiled up into Deputy Collins dark brown eyes.

"Well, I thought maybe I could interview you," Jake said hopefully.

"I think we're done here, don't you, Jake?" Sarah said looking him directly in the eyes and making her point crystal clear. "Deputy Collins, please let me take you to breakfast and thank you properly," Sarah commanded looking back at the handsome officer.

"Well, that would be nice, Miss McCaffrey. But I am still on duty," he said.

"Oh," Sarah said sounding a bit crest fallen. "Another time, then," she said trying to smile.

"Well, my shift ends at three o'clock. Why don't I treat you to dinner? I insist," he said, his face turning a bit red.

"Sounds wonderful," she grinned as she took his arm and walked past Jake who stood with his mouth hanging wide open.

"Don't catch any flies," I said as I playfully lifted his chin to close his mouth with my hand. "Better luck next time!" I laughed as Cassandra and I walked slowly up the hill behind Sarah and Deputy Collins.

Lincoln rushed up next to us, his face ashen. "We've got another emergency," he said as he rushed past us. "It's Olivia!"

"What's going on?" Cassandra asked as we all ran to follow Lincoln over to the tent.

"There's been some sort of accident with Miss Rivers. We got a radio report from your husband that Miss Rivers and her horse have had an accident on the trail near Devil's Falls," Sheriff Anderson informed us.

"Shane is there with her? Is he okay?" I was truly starting to panic.

"He's fine, Mrs. Spencer. Miss River's Horse slipped on the trail and she was thrown. She's stuck on some sort of ledge right now."

"Get me to her, right away!" Lincoln demanded.

"I can't, Detective. That trail has been washed out and about the only way to get there is on horseback. I'm not going to allow you to ride out there and risk injuring yourself," he told him.

"This my fiancé we are talking about," Lincoln informed

him. "I'm not going to wait around here and do nothing!"

"What about reaching her by helicopter?" Sarah suggested. "Could you drop a basket down and pull her up?"

"Sarah, you are a genius!" Cassandra declared.

"I think that will work," Sheriff Anderson agreed. "I'll radio my pilot with the coordinates."

"Radio your pilot to come get me. I want to be there to make sure everything goes smoothly," Lincoln stated. "I have helicopter rescue training. I was a Green Beret."

"Wow, Lincoln! I never knew that about you!" Sarah said with awe in her voice.

"There's a lot about Lincoln that we didn't know," Cassandra smiled and added. "Go get her, Detective!" she said and hugged him. "Be careful with our girl!"

"You know I will be!" he reassured her.

FOURTEEN

*D*an, the farmhands from River Bend Ranch, and the rest of the volunteers on horseback were returning to the parking lot. Cassandra, Sarah and I rushed over to speak with Dan, hoping to get an update on Olivia.

"Dan, what in the world happened?" I breathlessly asked as I rushed up to his horse.

"Well, from what your husband reported on the radio, Olivia decided to explore one of the more remote trails. She didn't want to leave any stone unturned to find Imogene and Sarah," Dan explained and nodded in Sarah's direction. "I'm glad you're okay m'am. We heard over the radio that you were missing as well."

"Thank you Dan, and thank you to all the volunteers who were looking for us," Sarah beamed.

"What happened to Olivia, Dan?" Cassandra urged, visibly upset.

"Well, we got the call over the radio from Shane that her horse, Maggie May, lost her footing, slipped and Olivia fell from the saddle."

"That doesn't sound like Olivia," I said.

"Well, she took the Devil's Falls trail. It's pretty muddy around that area and the trail is very rocky," he said. "There have been quite a few hikers over the years that had accidents on that trail."

"Didn't Sherriff Anderson tell the riders to stay off the trail?" I questioned Dan. "And my husband went willingly along with this?"

"Knowing Olivia, I don't think Shane had much of a choice," Cassandra reminded me. "He probably went with her to keep an eye on her."

"Amelia, Shane is all right. He stayed behind with Olivia. I hear she's pretty bruised and bumped up. She fell a good twenty feet, but she sure was lucky to land on that ledge," he said.

"We could have lost our girl," Cassandra said and her eyes filled with tears. "Why didn't she listen to Sheriff Anderson's warning? When I see her...I'm going to give her an earful!" Cassandra threatened.

"Here's your opportunity," Sarah said smiling, looking up as the helicopter appeared high in the midmorning sky.

"Oh, thank goodness!" Cassandra wailed and ran towards the command tent.

"Sheriff Anderson, Sheriff Anderson!" Cassandra called out. "Is she okay?"

"The rescue went without a hitch. We're flying her over to Johnson City Medical Center to let the doctors take a look at her as a precaution. Don't worry. She's going to be just fine!" Sheriff Anderson reassured me and patted Cassandra's back.

"That detective friend of yours sure knows his stuff!" the sheriff said.

"You're husband is on his way back with Maggie May, Amelia," Dan reminded us.

"Oh, thank goodness! This has been such a strange and bizarre twist of events," I sighed.

"I think we should get over to the hospital and check on Olivia, don't you?" Sarah suggested.

"I'd be happy to have one of my deputies give you a ride," Sheriff Anderson volunteered.

"Thank you, Sheriff, but I have my car parked right here," Cassandra informed him.

"I think I'll stay and wait to make sure Shane gets back okay," I told them. "I'll find you at the Medical Center just as soon as I can." I was beginning to worry about what was taking Shane so long. He was out in the woods by himself and was leading back a mare who might also be injured from the accident on the trail.

"Mrs. Spencer, I believe the rest of your rescue team has made it back safely," sheriff Anderson smiled and saw the worry evaporate from my face.

"Shane! Shane! Oh, gosh, you worried me!" I shouted as I flew across the parking lot. I was so relieved to see him, but my relief was soon replaced with anger. "What in the world were you doing riding along Devil's Falls? Didn't you and Olivia listen to the sheriff's warnings?"

"Well, I'm glad to see you too, sweetheart!" he teased and dismounted his horse. He wrapped his arms around me and held me in a long embrace.

"How's Maggie May?" Sarah asked as she joined us. She stooped down and began examining Maggie's legs for signs of injuries.

"She seems a little lame in her left rear leg, but I'm sure a little TLC out at Riverbend Ranch and she'll be fine. That was the oddest thing I ever saw. The path suddenly turned to mud and Maggie May and Olivia started to slide. Maggie held on as best she could, but Olivia toppled over her side."

"Oh, my gosh, Shane! That must have been horrible!" Sarah gasped and placed her hand up to her mouth.

"Hey Shane! Glad you made it back okay," Dan said as he approached our small group. He shook Shane's hand, and tipped his hat back to take a closer look at the horses.

"I think Maggie is a bit lame in her back left leg," Shane told Dan.

Dan carefully rubbed Maggie's left side and gently guided his hand down her leg. He gingerly felt up and down, and lifted her leg to examine her hoof.

"Is she okay?" I asked Dan.

"Other than some bruises and a few lacerations, she'll be fine. She'll just need to take it easy for a while," he reassured me and smiled. "I'll load her up and get her back home."

"Both Maggie May and her owner need to take it easy for a while," Cassandra snorted and crossed her arms. "She nearly scared me to death this time! She's lucky to be alive!"

"Thanks for everything, Dan, and for bringing the farmhands to help look for my Aunt. I can't thank you enough," I told him.

"It was our pleasure. We'll see y'all out at the ranch soon. Thanks, Shane. Come out for a trail ride at the ranch. You're a natural!"

"Yeah. Next time I think we'll stick to better traveled trails," he joked and patted Dan on the arm again.

"Shane, I'd like to head over to Johnson City Medical Center and check on Imogene and Olivia now," I told him. "Cassandra has volunteered to drive us over."

"Yes, let's head over there. She took a pretty big tumble off Maggie May. She's bound to be pretty banged up. I would feel better if I knew she was okay," he admitted.

"The car's right over here. Let's go!" I urged and led the way to Cassandra's Mercedes.

FIFTEEN

"Knock, knock!" Cassandra called out as we barged into Olivia's hospital room. Lincoln was by her side, gently running his fingers through Olivia's hair and kissing her forehead tenderly. The large emerald ring was visible on her ring finger and though her face was bruised and scratched, she had never looked happier!

"Olivia Rivers! You nearly scared us to death!" Cassandra chastised her. "Why can't you just do what you are told? What in the world made you decide to ride on the Devil's Falls trail?"

"Oh, I'm so glad to see all of you," she said and struggled to sit up in the hospital bed.

"Don't you move a muscle, my love," Lincoln reminded her. "You've got a couple of cracked ribs and the doctor wants you to be still and let the sedative help you sleep."

"There is no way I'm going to sleep after this little adventure! I've got too much to share with everyone," she smiled around the room at the group of us gathered around her bedside.

"Well…get on with it! I want details!" Cassandra barked.

"First, I need to know if Maggie May is all right," Olivia looked at Shane to answer.

"Other than a few scratches, Dan says she'll be fine in no time," Shane tried to reassure her.

"Shane Spencer… Are you telling me the truth? That was quite a slippery trail and it's not like Maggie to lose her footing like that. She tried her best to stay on the trail."

"It's so typical of you to worry more about your horse than yourself," Cassandra spoke up.

"She's my baby. I've raised her since she was a filly. She did her best to keep me safe. It's my fault that she even got the least bit injured," Olivia replied.

"Does that mean you'll listen next time and not take unnecessary chances?" Sarah challenged Olivia.

"Look who's talking *Laura Croft Tomb Raider!* When you found that opening, you should have gone for help," Olivia shot back. "Lincoln filled me in on what happened in the tunnel. You're lucky to be alive!"

"And so are you," Lincoln told his fiancé. "No more risks, ok? I can't have my finace risking her life!"

"And aren't you the pot calling the kettle black?" Olivia laughed at Lincoln. "I look up and there he is being lowered in a rescue basket, risking his life to save me. It was more romantic than *An Affair To Remember.*"

"I didn't even know you liked movies like that," Cassandra teased. "Olivia, you are much more romantic than I ever realized!"

"I love *An Affair To Remember* especially when Cary Grant realizes that she's the woman in the wheelchair who bought the painting," Sarah sighed.

"Okay enough about the movie and back to the proposal," Cassandra cut her off.

"Well, Lincoln wouldn't give the signal to the pilot to lift the basket until I accepted his proposal," Olivia smiled up at her handsome detective and squeezed his hand. "I had no choice but to accept his offer or I'd still be out on that ledge," she teased.

"I just wanted you to realize that it's okay to depend on someone else. It doesn't make you a weaker person, just a happier one! And I for one, my dear, intend to make you the happiest woman on the face of the earth!"

"I think I need a tissue," I said as my eyes welled up with tears.

"Here you go, Amelia," Sarah said grabbing one from her messenger bag. "In fact, I think we need tissues all around!" she cried and handed out tissues to all of us who were beaming and crying at the same time.

"I hate to break up this reunion," a charge nurse spoke from the doorway. "Miss Rivers needs to get some rest now!"

"Of course, of course! Sorry Liv!" I said and went to the opposite side of the bed and very gently hugged her. "Get some rest and we'll see you in the morning."

"Congratulations, Liv!" Sarah added. "You're going to be a beautiful bride," she said and kissed her friend's cheek.

"Thank you Sarah," Olivia beamed up at her good friend.

"Lincoln, tell her I mean it," Shane extended his hand and shook it enthusiastically. "I'm glad to know we'll be spending more time together."

"Indeed we will, Shane. I'm looking forward to it!"

"Liv, you've got one heck of a guy here! Congratulations! Shane said and squeezed Olivia's hand. "I'm glad everything worked out," he winked at her.

"You were right, Shane," Olivia agreed.

"Right about what?" Lincoln asked.

"Oh, Shane tried to tell me we were perfect for each other and basically not to be so headstrong," she sheepishly admitted.

"We ALL told you that," Cassandra added. "Lincoln, get over here and give me a hug!" Cassandra cried, weeping openly. "Welcome to the family and you better take care of our girl!"

"Cassandra, you know I will," he hugged her and lifted her off her feet and swung her around.

"Listen, you brute! Put me down before you break one of my ribs," she said playfully.

"Oh, you two stop! It hurts me to laugh! Ouch!" Olivia grabbed her ribs and tried to stop laughing at the scene taking place before her.

"We'll have plenty of time to plan a wedding after you're better. I told Lincoln already, but Doug and I would love to host your wedding at the lake house. Think about it and I will contact my event planner to get working on this!"

"I'm sure you'll have the whole wedding planned before your feet hit the parking lot," Olivia teased. "Cassandra, I don't want anything elaborate. Just a small wedding with family and friends."

"Right, a small wedding," Cassandra agreed. "I'll take care of all the details!"

"Cassandra... I mean it! Small means less than 30 people."

"La, la, la, la, la! I can't hear you!" she joked and walked out the door.

"Lincoln. Tell her I mean it," Olivia beseeched him.

"She's your friend," he smirked. "What do you want me to do? Get in the way of a beautiful friendship?"

"Cassandra!" Olivia cried.

"It's good to see I can still push her buttons," Cassandra laughed as we walked down the hospital corridor. "She'll let me have it tomorrow."

"I'm glad she's okay. I'm going to take a peek into Imogene's room before we leave," I told the girls.

"Knowing Imogene, she'll be entertaining the entire hospital staff," Shane predicted.

"Here's her room. I'll just knock gently and see if she's up to receiving visitors," I whispered as I approached her door.

"Ms. Smith has gone to sleep for the evening," a friendly nurse behind the desk informed us. "Are you family?"

"Yes, I'm her niece, Amelia Spencer," I informed her.

"We had to give your aunt a sleep aide. She was pretty wound up from the past few days events and the police questioned her extensively,"

"Oh, I hadn't thought about that. She must be exhausted!" Shane said to me.

"Well, actually, I think all the tweets and text messages she got were tiring her. I've never seen anything like it," the young brunette nurse admitted.

"You just don't know my Aunt Imogene," I grinned and looked around at my friends for confirmation.

"Her aunt is one-in-a-million!" Cassandra added. "Please tell her we came by,"

"I sure will!" the nurse said.

"When will she be allowed to go home?" I inquired.

"Tomorrow morning. The doctor is just keeping her here overnight for observation, but she's doing just fine!"

"Well, I'll be back in the morning to take her home," I told her.

"Come on Amelia! Let's head back to the Carnegie. I think we all could use a good night's sleep after our latest adventure," Cassandra suggested.

"I'm going to sleep like a baby now that I know Lucy is innocent, Imogene is safe and sound and Olivia finally has her prince charming," Sarah spoke up.

"Speaking of prince charming, don't you have dinner plans with a certain police officer?" I reminded her.

"Oh, my gosh! I completely forgot!" Sarah squeeled! "What time is it?" she grabbed her wrist and shook her head. "He'll be there in less than an hour!"

"That's just enough time to do a little fairy godmother magic and get you out of these jeans and sweatshirt. Wait until I'm done with you! Let's go raid my wardrobe!" Cassandra said gleefully.

SEVENTEEN

"I'm so glad you are back at Lyla's and everything is back to normal," I told Lucy as we enjoyed a bowl of her Greek lemon and rice soup. "This is so delicious! You'll have to share the recipe with me."

"No can do, Amelia!" Sarah joked. "Her soup recipe is what started this whole fiasco with Cheryl in the first place!"

"Poor, Cheryl," Lucy said shaking her head. "She thought she held all the cards by blackmailing Councilman Pete Johnson."

I took another sip of formosa oolong tea. I deeply inhaled and relaxed, so glad to have the recent events of the past few days behind us.

"This tea is excellent, Lucy!" Sarah smiled and looked around the table. She seemed very happy and confident.

"It's from Smoky Mountain Coffee, Herb and Tea Company. It's formosa oolong. I really like it!" Lucy added.

"Formosa what?" Lincoln asked.

"Formosa oolong," I repeated. "Formosa means beautiful island in Taiwanese."

"Formosa Olivia," Lincoln said and kissed his fiancé's hand, now adorned with the gorgeous emerald engagement ring.

"Lincoln, you're so bad," Olivia cooed.

"Get a room, you two!" Shane teased. "You two act like you're newlyweds."

"Not quite newlyweds," Cassandra spoke up, "But they're working on it. Let's talk wedding plans," she said and rubbed her hands together with anticipation.

"I think Lincoln and I have decided to get married at Riverbend Ranch," Olivia informed us. "I hope you don't mind, Cassandra, but I would like to ride up to the ceremony on horseback. It just makes sense to do it there," she said and leaned towards Cassandra.

"I think it makes perfect sense," Cassandra agreed. "It suits you. You'll just have to let me throw your rehearsal dinner party at my place!" she suggested. "You know the cocktails will be good!"

"Sounds perfect. Thank you, Cassandra!" Olivia hugged her. She seemed so happy and I was relieved that everything had turned out so well for these two.

"I do have a favor to ask you, though, Cassandra?"

"Anything, Olivia! Did you want to use my event planner?" Cassandra asked excitedly pulling her cell phone out and scrolling her contact list.

"No… No," Olivia said smiling.

"You want to hire my caterer, then, to do an over the top menu? Maybe a black tie cocktail reception with heavy h'ordeourvs?" Cassandra suggested?

"No. That's not what I wanted to ask you," Olivia stated.

"You want Vera Wang to design your gown? Or maybe I could call in a favor with Pnina Tornai!"

"Cassandra. Listen to me. I don't want your event planner's

number, your caterer's number or whatever a Panini is," Olivia interrupted her.

"Honey, a Panini is a grilled sandwich. Pnina Tornai is one of the most well known haute couture wedding dress designers in the world! You know, you've seen her on *Say Yes To The Dress!*"

"I don't care who she is," Olivia responded. "What I wanted to know was if you would be my matron of honor?" Olivia asked quickly.

"Will I be your matron of honor? Of course I will!" Cassandra shouted and jumped up from the table. She hugged Olivia from behind her chair and yelled in her ear. "Can I still plan the rehearsal dinner?"

"Yes, you can plan the rehearsal dinner. I just wanted to be sure that I am surrounded by all the people I love the most in the world. That's why I would like Amelia and Sarah to also be my maid and matron of honor too!"

"Oh, I'd be honored!" Sarah gasped!

"There's nothing I would rather love to do, Liv!" I answered and we all stood up and hugged.

"And while we're at it, Shane, I would like to ask if you would be my best man, since if it weren't for you, Olivia may not have accepted by offer," Lincoln joked.

"Of course, Matt. I'd be pleased to do that. Thanks!" Shane said.

"Well, I'm glad that all this drama has had a happy ending after all," Imogene piped up.

"Speaking of drama, so what is going to happen to Pete Johnson?" I asked Lincoln.

"Well, he's been charged with Cheryl's murder. The D.A. is seeking the death penalty," Lincoln stated seriously.

"And he's been charged with holding Sarah and myself as hostages," Imogene added. "I can't believe I ever voted for Pete Johnson. I should have known better," she said shaking her head.

"How could you have known what he was really like?" I reminded her. "At least he didn't get elected Mayor."

"Yeah, well Cheryl's sex tape with Pete threatened to undo his Mayorial Race. That man wasn't going to let her get in his way of his political aspirations," Imogene concluded.

"But how did you figure it out, Aunt Imogene?" Shane asked.

"It was the tax exemption documentation Delilah Bennett showed me on the Salt House. The papers had Pete Johnson's signature and when I went to the courthouse, I had Stella pull the legal notices for the Parson's Table. Pete Johnson was able to persuade the Historic Board to expedite the approval for Cheryl's tea room, the Parson's Table, and the Salt House to open. I knew she had someone pulling strings for her. It all added up!"

"So what happened on the bridge?" I asked, hoping Imogene was ready to talk about it.

"Well, I guess Stella has a mouth about as big as mine. She must have told someone and they tipped off Pete. When I got back in my car, I started to call you and tell you what I found out. I changed my mind when I realized it was almost time to meet you for dinner. I would just tell you in person. I started to drive slowly across the bridge, when out of nowhere, Pete suddenly jerked the car door open!"

"Oh, how terrible!" Sarah gasped. "That must have been so frightening!"

"It was. It was," Imogene agreed. "He had a gun and pointed it right in my face and told me to turn off the car and come with him. You should have seen the wild look in his eyes. He looked like he was crazy!"

"He must have been. He was crazy enough to murder at least one person," Olivia spoke up.

"So I did what he said." Imogene said reaching for another pita chip. "These are wonderfully tasty and crispy, Lucy."

"And then he took me into the tunnel," she continued.

"I never knew the tunnel even existed," Lucy said. "I've lived here my whole life and heard about how our area was split during the Civil War. There were many people who aided slaves with the Underground Railroad. I just never had an idea there was a tunnel right here under the streets of Jonesborough."

"Well, that's how Johnson was able to get from the bridge to the Court House so quickly the night he murdered Cheryl. The tunnel leads to the church right beside the Court House," Lincoln told us. "It was a very quick escape route for him. He had just enough time to remove his cape."

"Quick enough to make it in time for the Historical Board meeting," Lucy surmised. "And no one would be the wiser."

"And you just happened to be wearing a black hooded cape style coat. What a coincidence!" Sarah commented.

"Yes, quite a coincidence. If you hadn't figured out about that old tunnel, I still would be sitting in jail." Lucy patted Sarah's hand and squeezed it tight.

"Yes, how did you figure out about the tunnel?" Cassandra asked Sarah.

"Well, my infrared temperature gauge measured a drastic difference and I decided to take a look and investigate."

"I'm sorry I made fun of you for carrying around all those gizmos. You ended up finding Imogene with your thermometer," Olivia apologized.

"And that's when she stumbled upon the entrance to the tunnel," Imogene interrupted. "And thank goodness she came when she did!"

"Yes, thank goodness indeed!" I agreed.

"I could hear Pete Johnson yelling at Imogene. He was threatening to shoot her if she didn't tell him who else she had told about the court papers. He is such a terrible man!"

"And then, what?" Olivia asked on pins and needles.

"Well he yelled at me for hours. I knew just as soon as I told him the truth, he would kill me. He'd already killed once, so I knew he would do it again. I just refused to cooperate. He couldn't risk not finding out who also knew. So, he kept me alive just long enough for Sarah to show up."

"And then what happened?" Olivia spoke up impatiently.

"I was hiding in the shadows, watching what was going on. I was getting ready to turn and get help when I knocked a rock loose from along the tunnel wall. He heard the noise and came after me," Sarah said shaking. "I tried to hide, but the tunnel was too narrow. He laughed when he caught me and threw me down next to Imogene. He's a monster!"

"We found his black hooded cape in the tunnel," Lincoln testified. "It was covered with Cheryl's blood spatter. No attorney will be able to get him off with this much evidence. He'll be sentenced to life in prison without parole."

"You poor girls," Lucy spoke. "If I could get my hands on him right now…"

"You and me both," Imogene added. She began putting her lipstick on and grooming herself in her compact.

"Going somewhere?" I asked her.

"Well, as a matter-of-fact, I am! Sheriff Anderson is taking me to dinner," she said and winked at me.

"Yes, I noticed he seemed very concerned when you were missing," I teased her. "So how well do you know Sheriff Anderson?"

"Wouldn't you like to know!" Imogene cackled. "You'll just have to read my tweets! I'm off, you young people. Take care and come see me soon, Amelia!" Imogene said and air kissed my cheek.

"Goodby, Imogene! We can't let you leave without giving you a hug," Shane requested.

"You take good care of my niece and my great niece Emma and great nephew Charlie!" Imogene said and squeezed Shane tight. "I'm going to come for a visit real soon!"

"You do that, Imogene. We'd love to have you!" Shane replied.

"Bye, Imogene! You're one heck of a lady," Cassandra piped up.

"I'm sure glad my Amelia has such good friends," Imogene smiled and hugged everyone. "I know we will be seeing much more of each other!"

"You have a good time with Sheriff Anderson," Olivia

joked. "But not too much fun!"

"I'll see you at your wedding," she laughed and was out the door.

"What a lady!" Cassandra said.

"What a broad," Lincoln chuckled.

"Thank you girls, for all your help. I would still be rotting away in that jail cell if it were not for you," Lucy sincerely said.

"It was our pleasure, Lucy," Cassandra said.

"When you go through difficult times, you find out who your friends truly are," she continued. "We had our biggest weekend at Lyla's and I have you girls to thank for that!"

"Thank Darla. She was the real backbone of the team," Olivia reported. "That young lady not only can cook, she is a natural business woman!"

"Yes, my niece has really shown me how well she can run Lyla's. I'm thinking of turning the business over to her and doing some traveling myself!"

"Lucy! That's wonderful!" Cassandra encouraged her. "You deserve some down time."

"This whole ordeal has helped me realize that life is short and there are some things I would like to do while I can still do them," she added. "I've booked a trip to England at the end of this month."

"That sounds wonderful, Lucy! I hope you have a wonderful time," I hugged her.

"I thought I might try some authentic scones and tea room fare!"

"Oh, be sure to stop at the Lanesborough Hotel in Knightsbridge. It's across the street from Hyde's Park and it

has a delightful afternoon tea. One of the best, in my opinion," Cassandra strongly recommended. "The tea service is in a
beautiful conservatory full of exotic plants and has a wonderful
ambiance."

"Sounds charming! I can't wait! Amelia, you lived in London studying abroad. Where did you enjoy taking tea?" Lucy
inquired.

"I was on a student's budget, so my tea experiences were a
bit more simple than the Lanesborough Hotel. I did love going
to the market stalls and enjoying tea from small tea companies.
It's a wonderful way to see areas such as Picadilly Circus and
Knotting Hill," I told her wistfully.

"I just can't wait! Do you have any trips coming up, girls?"
Lucy asked.

"Do work related trips count?" Shane asked. "If they do,
then Savannah is our next trip."

"What's going on in Savannah?" Lucy asked.

"The Gourmet Fancy Foods Show will be held this year in
Savannah. Amelia and I are going to have a booth for Smoky
Mountain Coffee, Herb and Tea. This is our first major show,
so we are very excited!" Shane reported.

"Terrific!" Lucy cheered.

"Reynolds's Candies will be there as well right next to us,"
I added.

"Well, why not?" Cassandra commented. "It's good for
companies that promote 'Pick Tennessee' to stick together. Plus
we are partnering up for a cooking demo for our tea infused
truffles."

"Wow. I know I plan on going. I will be there ordering for

the Pink Dogwood Tea Room!" Sarah added. "We should have tea at the Savannah Tea Room if y'all can find time during the show.

"I think we can make that happen," Shane smiled and put his arm around me. He was looking forward to the Fancy Food Show. We had rented a large carriage house bordering Forsythe Park so we would be close to all the downtown attractions.

"We've got room for you to stay with us, Sarah, if you'd like. It's in the historic district," I added.

"Oh, that would be wonderful!" she beamed. "That way I could do the nighttime ghost walks in Savannah."

"Oh, good grief! Here we go again," Olivia sighed.

"After all that has happened, you still don't believe?" Sarah asked astonished.

"I didn't see any evidence of ghosts during our tour. So no, I still don't believe," Olivia informed her.

"Didn't you see *Midnight in the Garden of Good and Evil?*" Sarah asked. "That movie will make a believer out of you! It's all about ghosts and the dead in Savannah. It's based on a real murder and the trial of Jim Williams. Jude Law, Kevin Spacey and John Cusack starred in the movie. It's really fascinating."

"Well I'll have to go rent that one. I'm not very familiar with Savannah," Lincoln said.

"Haven't you been, Lincoln?" Olivia asked patting his knee.

"No, can't say I have. I haven't done much traveling around the Eastern part of the United States."

"Well maybe it's time you did! I for one would welcome a little male companionship in Savannah. We've got the room if you'd like to come!" Shane offered.

"I love it!" Cassandra rallied. "Another trip for 'The Traveling Tea Ladies!'" She raised her tea cup in a salute and we all gently clinked tea cups.

"To 'The Traveling Tea Ladies!'" I cheered.

"To us!" Sarah joined.

"To us!" Olivia said and kissed Lincoln full on the mouth.

"To the girls!" Shane laughed and clinked his tea cup with Lincoln.

We were ready for our next adventure!

~THE END~

How to Make
the Perfect Pot of Tea

In the same amount of time that you measure level scoops of coffee for the coffee maker and add ounces of water, you can prepare a cup or pot of tea.

Step 1: Select your tea pot.

Porcelain or pottery is the better choice versus silver plated tea pots which can impart a slightly metallic taste. Make sure your tea pot is clean with no soapy residue and prime your tea pot by filling it with hot water, letting it sit for a few minutes and then pouring the water out so that your pot will stay warm longer!

Step 2: WATER, WATER, WATER!

Begin with the cleanest, filtered, de-chlorinated water you can. Good water makes a huge difference. Many of my tea room guests have asked why their tea doesn't taste the same at home. The chlorine in the water is often the culprit of sabotaging a great pot of tea.

Be sure your water comes to a rolling boil and quickly remove it. If you let it boil continuously, you will boil out all the oxygen and be left with a "flat" tasting tea. Please do not microwave your water. It can cause your water to "super boil" and lead to third degree burns. If you are in a situation where you don't have a full kitchen, purchase an electric tea kettle to quickly and easily make your hot water.

And NEVER, NEVER, EVER MAKE TEA IN A COFFEE MAKER! I cannot tell you how I cringe when asked if it's okay. Coffee drinkers don't want to taste tea and tea drinkers don't want to taste coffee. Period! End of story! Golden rule—no coffee makers!

Now that we've cleared that up, let's measure out our tea!

Step 3: Measure Out Your Tea.

It's easy! The formula is one teaspoon of loose tea per 8 ounces of water. For example, if you are using a 4 cup teapot, you would use 4 teaspoons of tea, maybe a little less depending on your personal taste. Measure your tea and place inside a "t-sac" or paper filter made for tea, infuser ball, or tea filter basket. Place the tea inside your pot and now you're ready for steeping.

Step 4: Steeping Times and Temperature.

This is the key!

Black teas—Steep for 3-4minutes with boiling water (212 degrees)

Herbals, Tisanes and Rooibos—boiling water, Steep for 7 minutes.

Oolongs—195 degree Water. Steep for 3 minutes.

Whites and Greens—Steaming water—175 degrees. Steep for 3 minutes.

Over steeping any tea will make your tea bitter! Use a timer and get it right. Using water that is too hot for whites and greens will also make your tea bitter!

Got Milk?

Many tea drinkers are under the misconception that cream should be added to your tea, not milk. Actually cream and half-n-half are too heavy. Milk can be added to most black teas and to some oolongs. I don't recommend it for herbals, greens and whites.

The debate continues as to whether to pour milk into your cup before your tea or to add milk after you pour your tea. Really, the decision is yours! I always recommend tasting your tea first before adding milk or any sugar. You would be surprised how perfectly wonderful many teas are without any additions. I think you're ready to start your tea adventure!

Until Our Next Pot of Tea,

Melanie

Recipes From
The Traveling Tea Ladies
–Death in Dixie

Charlie's Blueberry Almond Sour Cream Pie

"I'll have to make sure I have plenty of peach iced tea ready and an extra large slice of blueberry almond sour cream pie to thank her," Sarah said laughing. Olivia was a hard worker, a good friend, and was famous for her ravenous appetite and sassy attitude to match her auburn hair. –Chapter One

2 unbaked deep dish pie crusts

2 cups sour cream

2 eggs

1 ½ cup sugar

½ cup flour

1 ½ teaspoon almond extract

4 cups fresh blueberries or frozen blueberries

2 tablespoons flour

Topping:

1 cup flour

1 stick butter

2/3 cup sliced almonds

1/3 cup sugar

Directions: Mix all filling ingredients, except blueberries. Toss the blueberries and two tablespoons flour, gently. Fold floured blueberries into sour cream mixture. Pour into both piecrusts. Bake at 350 degrees until filling is just setting, usually 30 minutes.

For Topping: Using a food processor, pulse flour, butter and sugar until crumbly. Add sliced almonds and pulse briefly. Or the old fashioned method using a pastry cutter to cut the butter works well.

Sprinkle topping over tops of pies and bake another 12-15 minutes. Allow pies to cool to room temperature. Be sure to refrigerate left overs, but don't worry— you won't have much left!

Note From Melanie: This is my son Charlie's favorite pie recipe. He requests it every Fourth of July and anytime fresh blueberries are in season. I love this pie served with a dollop of my almond cream. The recipe for almond cream can be found in *The Traveling Tea Ladies–Death in Dallas.*

Smoky Mountain Sweet Potato Scones

"Why don't we take a break and reward ourselves for all this hard work," Sarah said and put her arm across my shoulders. "I have a batch of sweet potato scones that I baked this morning which would be perfect with a pot of the new spice Ceylon tea you brought over." –Chapter One

2-1/4 cups all-purpose flour

1/4 cup packed brown sugar

2 teaspoons baking powder

1-1/2 teaspoons pumpkin pie spice

3/4 teaspoon salt

1/4 teaspoon baking soda

1/3 cup cold butter

1 egg, lightly beaten

1 cup mashed sweet potatoes

1/3 cup buttermilk

In a large bowl, combine the flour, brown sugar, baking powder, pumpkin pie spice, salt and baking soda. Cut in butter until mixture resembles coarse crumbs. In a small bowl, whisk the egg, sweet potatoes and buttermilk; add to dry ingredients just until moistened.

On a well floured surface, gently roll out dough to a ½ inch thickness. Flour a round biscuit cutter. Gently push biscuit cutter straight down into dough and lift straight up. Do not twist cutter as that will break the air bubbles in the dough and you will not have a scone that rises high when baked. Place on baking sheet covered in parchment paper or place on a silicone baking sheet. Sprinkle with cane sugar for a sweet and crunchy topping. Bake in a preheated 400 degree oven for 23-25 minutes until slightly brown on top. Serve hot or warm with a dollop of lemon curd.

Note From Melanie: There are many variations to traditional scone recipes. This one happens to be one of my favorites that I look forward to baking during the fall and holiday season. A batch of these scones will make your kitchen small like grandma came for a visit!

Luscious Lemon Curd

She quickly moved about the kitchen, placing two beautiful sweet potato scones on Wedgewood autumn vine plates, adding small ramekins filled with homemade lemon curd and apple butter to accompany them. The aromas in the kitchen were intoxicating.–Chapter One

5 eggs

1 cup granulated sugar

4 lemons, zested and juiced

1 stick butter, chilled and cut into small pieces

In a medium sized saucepan, add approximately one inch of water. Bring to a simmer over medium heat. In the meantime, locate a metal bowl that is large enough to fit in the top of the saucepan without touching the water (must be metal). In the metal bowl, combine egg yolks and sugar and whisk for one minute until smooth. Add cut up butter, zest and lemon juice. Once water reaches a simmer in the saucepan, reduce heat to low and place bowl on top of saucepan. Continually whisk lemon mixture until thickened, approximately 20 minutes or until mixture is light yellow and coats the back of a wooden spoon. Remove promptly from heat and allow to cool at room temperature for 2 hours. Place lemon curd in airtight sealable containers and refrigerate for 6 hours before serving. Can be kept refrigerated for up to 2 weeks.

Note From Melanie: Store bought lemon curd cannot hold a candle to homemade. Lemon curd takes time to make, but is worth the effort! This decadent treat is a must-have with scones, but is so wonderful, it can be a base for desserts too. I like to fill miniature phyllo cups with lemon curd, top with homemade whipped cream or almond cream and garnish with a slice of strawberry, blueberry or a raspberry for a refreshing tea time treat. Lemon curd is lovely on raisin toast, as a dip for fresh strawberries, as a filling for trifle and any other dreamy treat your imagination can pair it with!

The Pink Lady Cream of Tomato Soup

"I think she is pushy. It's amazing what people will ask you and expect you to answer like what's the secret ingredient in your signature cream of tomato soup or can they have the recipe? If you share it, it won't be special anymore," I reminded her. –Chapter One

> 4 Tablespoons butter or olive oil
> 1 small onion, finely chopped
> 2 tablespoons minced garlic
> 1 large can tomato juice
> 1 cup heavy whipping cream, ½ n ½ or whole milk
> Salt and Pepper to taste

Melt butter or heat oil on medium heat in a medium size stockpot. Add onion and cook until translucent, about 2-3 minutes. Add garlic and continue cooking on medium heat for a few minutes, being careful not to burn it. Once garlic is cooked, pour can of tomato juice into stockpot and turn up heat until the soup boils. Reduce heat to medium and cover with lid. Allow soup to simmer for about 15 minutes. Reduce heat to low and add cream, salt and pepper to taste.

Note From Melanie: I like to serve this soup in individual tea cups. For a pretty presentation, I garnish with chives and sour cream.

Lyla's Blue Ribbon Pumpkin Bisque

Lucy came back by the table with steaming bowls of pumpkin bisque and a pot of tea. She sat down, her hands visibly trembling. –Chapter Two

1/4 cup butter

1 small onion, chopped

1 14.5 ounce container of chicken broth

1 15 ounce can pumpkin pie mix

1 12 ounce can evaporated milk

1/8 teaspoon cinnamon

Melt butter. Add chopped onion. Cook over medium heat until onion is soft, about 2-3 minutes. Add broth and bring to a boil. Reduce heat to low and cook for 15 minutes. Stir in pumpkin pie mix, evaporated milk and cinnamon. Cook for 5 more minutes. Transfer mixture to food processor. Pulse mixture until smooth. Return to sauce pan and heat. Serve warm with a dollop of sour cream and sprinkle of cinnamon.

Note From Melanie: This soup was one of my many "whoops" in the tea room! I mistakenly picked up pumpkin pie mix instead of 100% pumpkin. I didn't have enough time to run to the store before our lunch rush, so I had to make due with what I had on hand. The soup ended up being a favorite and one of our most requested. I never went back to the original recipe after that fateful day. I hope you enjoy it as much as our Miss Melanie's Tea Room guests did!

Amelia's Baked Acorn Squash

We walked over to the large knotty pine trestle table on the stone patio and I began unpacking my contribution of baked squash with brown sugar and raisins as I retold the day's events in Jonesborough. –Chapter Three

2 large acorn squash
4 Tablespoons butter
    Raisins
4 Tablespoons brown sugar

Prick acorn squash with fork over entire surface. Place in microwave and bake for 5-7 minutes. This will precook the squash and make it easier to cut in half. Cut bottoms off of acorn squash so they will sit flat. Be careful not to take too much off as this will cause butter mixture to leak out during baking. Cut squash into two halves and scoop out seeds and stringy pulp.

Place squash in oven safe dish face up. Place 1 Tablespoon of butter and 1 Tablespoon brown sugar into each half. Add raisins as desired. Bake in preheated oven at 400 degrees for 25 minutes or until squash is soft and brown sugar filling is bubbly.

Note From Melanie: This recipe is a great way to get kids to try squash. My Mom always made this on meatloaf nights in the fall and we devoured it and always wanted more! Also a great Thanksgiving side dish. If you are feeding a crowd, you can cut squash into segments and serve to feed more. A beautiful presentation on any table.

Cassandra's Tea-Tinis

"Here, Liv. Have a sip of this "Tea-tini."Cassandra said and slid a glass towards her. –Chapter Three

1 ¾ ounce vodka

1 ounce sweet iced tea

¼ ounce lemon juice, freshly squeezed lemon wedge

for garnish

Fill cocktail shaker with ice. Pour all ingredients into cocktail shaker. Shake well and pour into chilled martini glasses. Garnish with lemon wedge.

Note From Melanie: To make this drink over-the-top, run lemon wedge around edge of martini glass. Dip rim into sugar. This is a wonderful beverage on a warm summer's night.

Main Street Wild Rice and Mushroom Soup

"I can't begin to tell you how much I appreciate every-thing you girls are doing to help me!" Lucy told us as we were seated around a large round table enjoying a salad and her new soup of the day–wild rice and mushroom. –Chapter Five

1 pint fresh mushroom, cleaned and stems cut off

½ stick butter

2 Tablespoons fresh garlic, minced

1 small onion, chopped

2 cups chicken broth or chicken stock

½ uncooked wild rice

1 cup heavy whipping cream or half-n-half

Salt and pepper to taste

In a large stock pot, heat butter at medium heat until barely melted. Do not allow to brown! Add onion and cook until translucent. Add garlic and mushrooms and cook until mushrooms are tender. Add chicken broth/stock and rice and bring to a boil. Cover pot with lid and reduce heat to low and allow soup to simmer for 20 minutes. Turn off heat and add cream. Salt and pepper to taste and serve immediately.

Note From Melanie: This soup is decadent, creamy, satisfying and a popular request among my tea room guests. My husband, Keith, also requests this soup on a regular basis. Once you serve this selection, expect it to be a much anticipated favorite at gatherings and home. Enjoy!

Treasure Island Rum Raisin Scones

"Two trifles and two orders of rum raisin scones, please Darla!" Cassandra called cheerily back to the kitchen. "Amelia, can you help me make a couple pots of tea?" –Chapter Eight

2 cups all purpose flour

2 teaspoons baking powder

½ teaspoon salt

1 stick unsalted butter

¼ cup sugar

½ cup raisins

2 Tablespoons rum extract or rum

2 eggs

Heavy whipping cream, approximately ¼ cup

1 Tablespoon vanilla extract

Cane sugar for topping

In a small mixing bowl, place raisins and combine with rum extract or rum, if you choose. Allow raisins to rehydrate by soaking in liquid while completing other steps in preparing scones.

In a chilled large mixing bowl, stir together flour, baking powder, sugar and salt. Cut in butter with a cold pastry blender until mixture resembles coarse crumbs.

Drain liquid from raisins. Add raisins to flour mixture and toss to coat.

In a small bowl, whisk together eggs and vanilla. Add to flour mixture to combine. Slowly pour in heavy whipping cream adding a little at a time until mixture is sticky and dough forms. Eyeball it and add just enough to moisten dough. You may use less than ¼ cup or a little bit more depending on the day's humidity and other factors.

On a well floured surface, gently roll out dough to a ½ inch thickness. Flour a round biscuit cutter. Gently push biscuit cutter straight down into dough and lift straight up. Do not twist cutter as that will break the air bubbles in the dough and you will not have a scone that rises high when baked. Place on baking sheet covered in parchment paper or place on a silicone baking sheet. Sprinkle with cane sugar for a sweet and crunchy topping. Bake in a preheated 400 degree oven for 23-25 minutes until slightly brown on top. Serve hot or warm with a dollop of lemon curd.

Note From Melanie: I came up with this recipe when I was putting together a themed tea tray for our *Treasure Island* themed afternoon tea. Needless to say, the guests love the scones with raisins soaked in rum best and it was a nice change from a traditional scone.

Lucy's Greek Lemon And Rice Soup

"I'm so glad you are back at Lyla's and everything is back to normal," I told Lucy as we enjoyed a bowl of her Greek lemon and rice soup. "This is so delicious! You'll have to share the recipe with me." –Chapter Sixteen

6 cups chicken broth

¾ cup uncooked long grain rice

2 cups cooked chicken breast, shredded

2 large room temperature eggs

1/3 cup fresh sqeezed lemon juice

1 lemon sliced thinly

In a stock pot, heat the chicken stock and uncooked rice until it reaches a boil. Reduce heat to medium low and bring the liquid to a simmer. Cover and cook until rice is cooked— about 15 minutes. Add chicken. Remove the soup from the heat. Ladle 1 cup hot broth from the soup pot and slowly add it to the eggs, whisking continually using a tempering method. Slowly stir the egg mixture back into the soup. Ladle the soup into individual bowls and garnish with sliced lemon.

Note From Melanie: This soup is light, satisfying, and low fat. To make it even healthier, use low sodium chicken broth. This is a great summer soup and takes me back to sharing Greek Orthodox Easter each year with our friends, the Ioannides in Miami, Florida.

Resource Guide

JONESBOROUGH, Tennessee's oldest town, is nestled between the Appalachian Mountains and the Great Smoky Mountains in the upper Northeast corner of the state bordering North Carolina and Virginia. Jonesborough has been named one of the top Main Streets in the U.S.A. and is host to the National Storytelling Festival held annually the first weekend in October. Recently, Jonesborough was featured as one of the locations on Food Network's *The Great Food Truck Race.*

I moved to Knoxville, Tennessee from Miami when I was just 13 years old and have been proud to call the Volunteer State "home." I opened my Johnson City tearoom, Miss Melanie's Tea Room, in November of 2005 in our 107 year old Victorian home. Although I closed the doors in 2010, I still enjoy teaching three day seminars at our tea room through our Tea Academy classes and am actively involved in our gourmet tea and coffee business, Smoky Mountain Coffee, Herb and Tea Company. And, I'm finding that the tea room makes a beautiful backdrop for writing books in *The Traveling Tea Ladies* series.

North east Tennessee abounds with nature, history and many activities besides the National Storytelling Festival. In this resource guide, I have included several of the dining, shopping, and tourist destinations mentioned in *The Traveling Tea Ladies–Death in Dixie*. I hope you will come visit our beautiful state and see some of these attractions for yourself. I think our down home southern roots and hospitality will make you feel right at home!

Apple Festival

Erwin, Tennessee. Located at the foot of the Appalachian Mountains held annually the first weekend in October in "the valley beautiful."

Local crafters, food and entertainment.

www.unicoicounty.org/applefest.php

Smoky Mountain Coffee, Herb & Tea Company

Official tea company of The Traveling Tea Ladies. A complete selection of the coffee and teas mentioned in the series are available for purchase.

www.SmokyMountainCoffee-Herb-Tea.com

National Storytelling Festival

Held annually the first weekend in October in historic Jonesborough, Tennessee. Storytellers from around the world participate in this event held in tents along Main Street. Passes for the three day event can be purchased at:

www.storytellingfestival.net

Pal's Sudden Service "Great food in a flash!"

Stand alone drive-thru chain known for it's "peachie" iced tea, "frenchie" fries, and thought of the day. Located in the Tricities, Tennessee area (Johnson City, Kingsport and Bristol).

www.palsweb.com

Massengill's

246 East Main Street, Johnson City, TN 37604. An upscale women's boutique in downtown historic Johnson City.

Dogwood and Cattail's Ball:

An annual event for pets and pet owners with proceeds benefitting the Humane Society of Washington County, Tennessee.

www.wchsus.com

Salt House

127 Fox Street Jonesborough, Tennessee 37659. Built in 1864, this historic building has served as a salt distribution site during the Civil War as well as a Masonic Hall, grocery store, gift shop and restaurant.

Parson's Table

102 West Woodrow Avenue Jonesborough, Tennessee 37659. This former church was once a famous restaurant in Jonesborough. It is now rented for private events. During the cholera epidemic, it served as a temporary storehouse for coffins.

Small Miracles Therapeutic Equestrian Center

1026 Rock Springs Drive, Kingsport, Tennessee

www.small-miracles.org (423) 349-1111

Abrams Falls

Near Townsend, Tennessee, one of the most beautiful hiking destinations in the Great Smoky Mountains National Park.

www.hikinginthesmokys.com/Abrams.htm

Tea Time Magazine

A must have periodical for tea room and tea lovers alike!

www.TeaTimeMagazine.com

Carnegie Hotel

1216 West State of Franklin Road, Johnson City, Tennessee, 37604. AAA four diamond property offering well appointed rooms in a baroque style decor. Be sure to visit the wine cellar in the lower level.

www.CarnegieHotel.com (423) 979-6400

Austin Springs Spa

1216 West State of Franklin Road, Johnson City, Tennessee 37604. Located on the bottom level of the Carnegie Hotel.

www.AustinSpringsSpa.com (423) 979-6403

International Storytelling Center

116 West Main Street, Jonesborough, Tennessee 37659.

www.storytellingcenter.net (423) 753-2171

Mini-Dome

Located on the campus of East Tennessee State University, this multi-purpose building can seat up to 8539 fans and is the site of many Buccaneer athletic games.

www.ETSU.edu

Jonesborough Court House

103 West Main Place, Jonesborough, Tennessee 37659. Built in 1779, this building stood in the capital of the State of Franklin, named in honor of Benjamin Franklin. Later, the State of Franklin would become the Tennessee Territory.

James D. Hoskins Library, University of Tennessee

1015 Volunteer Boulevard, Knoxville, Tennessee. Built in 1950, this building is named after the fourteenth President of U.T.

www.lib.utk.edu (865) 974-4480

Bistro 105

105 East Main Street, Jonesborough, Tennessee 37659. Famous for Chef Todd's fried green tomato BLTs.

(423) 788-0244

The Farmer's Daughter Restaurant

7700 Erwin Highway, Chuckey, Tennessee 37641. Down home country cooking served family style. A true southern dining experience.

www.farmersdaughterrestaurant.com (423) 257-4650

Appalachian Ghost Walk Tours

Nightly lantern guided tours year round featuring a tour of Jonesborough, named one of the top ten most haunted towns.

www.appalachianghostwalks.com (423) 743-WALK (9255)

Mona Lisa's Gelato

305 West Oakland Avenue, Suite #110, Johnson City, Tennessee 37604. Authentic Italian gelato with a diverse menu featuring soups, sandwiches, whoopie pies and cupcakes.

www.MonaLisasGelato.com (423) 262-8357

Jonesborough Visitors Center and Museum

117 Boone Street, Jonesborough, Tennessee 37659.

www.jonesboroughtn.org (423) 753-1345

Andrew Johnson National Historic Site

121 Monument Avenue, Greeneville, TN 37743. Come visit the homes, tailor shop, and gravesite of our 17th President located in Tennessee's second oldest town.

www.nps.gov/anjo (423) 638-3551

Follow The Quilt Trail

Step back in time and enjoy the scenic side of Northeast Tennessee as you enjoy the artistry of quilting displayed on historic barns scattered throughout the rolling countryside. Take a self-guided tour or sign up for a deluxe coach trip—the options are limitless.

www.quilttrail.org

Rocky Mount Museum A Living History Site

200 Hyder Hill Road, Piney Flats, Tennessee 37686-4630 Built in 1791, this structure served as home to William Blount as he served as Governor of the Southwest Territory under President George Washington. Come visit the kitchen building, spin yarn, or experience "wooly day" with demonstrations of shearing sheep.

(423) 538-7396

Bristol Caverns

1157 Bristol Caverns Highway, Bristol, Tennessee 37620. Over 200 million years old, this cave is home to an underground river as well as breathtaking stalactites and stalagmites. Open year round.

www.BristolCaverns.com   (423) 878-2011

Bays Mountain Park and Planetarium

853 Bays Mountain Park Road, Kingsport, Tennessee. Come visit the wolves! This 3500 acre nature reserve is also home to reptiles, raptors and bobcats. Have a hair raising adventure on the zip line, enjoy the 44 acre lake or visit the state-of-the-art planetarium.

www.BaysMountain.com (423) 229-9447

Gray Fossil Site

1212 Suncrest Drive, Gray, Tennessee 37615. Explore the world's largest tapir fossil find, see a complete skeleton of a Teleoceras or discover a new species of plant-eating badgers. The Gray Fossil Museum offers daily tours as well as special camps for kids who are interested in paleontology.

www.GrayFossilMuseum.com (423) 439-3659

Bristol Motor Speedway

2801 Highway 11 E Bristol, Tennessee. "It's probably the most intimidating track that you walk up to for a race weekend. The way it looks, the way it's shaped, the way you have to race there-it's its own unique animal. There's no place like it in the world like it." Kurt Busch

Built in 1960, this ½ mile concrete track is the fourth largest sports venue in America. Come for a race or visit during Christmas when the track is decked out in two million Christmas lights for its annual "Speedway in Lights" to benefit Bristol Speedway Children's Charities. Ice skating is also available during the months of December and January.

(423) 764-3724

A Letter to the Reader

Dear Friend,

    I often get asked when and how I began writing and I have to laugh thinking back to the plays I wrote to raise money for the Jerry Lewis Muscular Dystrophy Telethon. Instead of selling lemonade or a bake sale, I involved all the kids on our block in elaborate productions which we rehearsed for days. I soon learned that attention spans are short when you are seven years old and kids would rather ride bikes or play with their Barbie's instead of rehearse, so we never actually made it to the final performance. But I wrote one every summer and practiced all the parts myself, usually roping my brother, Greg, into it!

    Growing up, I always had a pot of tea with my mother after school and one of our favorite things to do when we traveled was to visit tea rooms. It was only after my summer living abroad in London studying international communications that I experienced authentic Afternoon Tea and my passion for tea was truly ignited! I knew I wanted to return to the states, open my own tea business and share my love of tea with everyone. Many years later, with much encouragement and support from my husband, Keith, and our children, the dream began with the opening of Miss Melanie's Tea Room, the addition of our online business- Smoky Mountain Coffee, Herb and Tea

Company and eventually expanding into consulting and training tea professionals all over the U.S. with The Tea Academy.

Many of the recipes I feature in this book are tried and true in my tea room and come from my grandmothers, Ellen and Essie. Grandma Ellen was a wonderful baker and her cheese cake was legendary as well as her cookies. My grandmother, Essie, actually owned her own restaurant and allowed me to take guest's orders at the early age of three! Of course, one of her servers was standing by to make sure the order was turned into the kitchen correctly, but I can vividly remember how exciting it was to visit her at her restaurant.

I hope you enjoy taking this journey with me and glimpsing life in a small East Tennessee town. It doesn't get much better than looking out your window at the splendor of autumn leaves in hues of burnt orange and gold; the panoramic view of the snow capped Smoky Mountains in winter or the countryside scattered with blooming Dogwoods and Redbud trees in the spring. I hope you will find a comfortable chair to snuggle up in, make a hot pot of tea or a pitcher of iced tea and join Amelia and her friends on their tea adventures!

I invite you to join our "Traveling Tea Ladies Society" and share your own personal tea adventures and photos with us! There will be opportunities for you to attend upcoming book signings, tea tastings, tea tours and more. Please visit www. TheTravelingTeaLadies.com to register for our newsletter or follow us on Facebook. I would love to hear from you!

Until Our Next Pot of Tea,

About the Author

 Melanie O'Hara-Salyers is a graduate of Southern Methodist University and East Tennessee State University. Her hobbies include travel, cooking for her large family, dancing, tea drinking, herb and flower gardening, reading and spending time with her husband, Keith, and their five children.

She enjoys working with local children, teaching etiquette and cooking through her "Kids in the Kitchen" classes and summer camps. Melanie also encourages children to develop a love of reading through her monthly "Literary Teas" that are based on classic novels such as *Little Women, Anne of Green Gables, Gone with the Wind* and *The Secret Garden.*

Melanie also shares her passion for tea with people inspired to follow their tea dreams. Participants in her Tea Academy seminars held across the U.S. and at her tea room, Miss Melanie's Tea Room, receive extensive training, tea education, and learn how to successfully own, operate, and promote their own tea businesses.

She is proud to call East Tennessee home. Her tea room, Miss Melanie's, and her online tea and coffee business, Smoky Mountain Coffee, Herb and Tea Company, is located in the heart of historic downtown Johnson City. If you would like to schedule a tea lecture, tea tasting, cooking demonstration, book signing or tea tour, please e-mail her at: Melanie@TheTravelingTeaLadies.com

About the Artist

Susi Galloway Newell

Fine Artist & Illustrator

Her artistic career started at the early age of 15 with formal studies and training in Heraldic Arts under a master.

Further inspired by old masters, fantasy and surrealists she broadened the scope of her career from Heraldic Art to Fine Art, Illustration and Design.

Her paintings reflect a fascination for medieval art, beautiful scenery, unique viewpoints, fantasy and illusions.

She works with traditional brush and paint and also paints digital.

She also enjoys bringing stories to life with vibrant and beautiful illustrations and specializes in children's books, character designs fantasy, sci-fi, mystery illustrations and cover art.

Born and raised in Switzerland, she loves travel, adventure, the outdoors and eclectic cultures.

Together with her husband Jim and dog Cosmo she has made Clearwater, Florida her permanent home.

For more info please visit: www.susigalloway.com

About the Photographer

As a regional and nationally respected fine art portrait photographer, David Clapp offers his gift of interpretive and sensitive imaging to clients from all over the country. David's background in both the arts and engineering assures his clients not only of technical excellence, but also offers the rare blend of merging the artist's eye with technology.

"Whether it's a baby, child, family, bride or professional, I consider it one of life's greatest joys to be part of leaving a legacy…through the lens."

David can be reached at his North East Tennessee studio by calling (423) 378-5044.

View his work at: www.DavidClapp.com

THE TEA ACADEMY

Consulting & Training for Tea Professionals

www.TheTeaAcademy.com

SMOKY MOUNTAIN COFFEE, HERB AND TEA COMPANY

www.SmokyMountainCoffee-Herb-Tea.com

Official Tea Company of the *Traveling Tea Ladies*

LYONS
LEGACY
PUBLISHING™

Traveling Tea Ladies readers, for other Lyons Legacy titles you may enjoy, or to purchase other books in The Traveling Tea Ladies Series, signed by the author, visit our website:

www.LyonsLegacyPublishing.com

Coming in 2011

The Traveling Tea Ladies
Death in the Low Country

Former tea room owner, Amelia Spencer, and her fun-loving friends are known about their small town of Dogwood, Tennessee as "The Traveling Tea Ladies" because everywhere their tea travels take them, murder and mayhem seem to follow. When the ladies participate in the Fancy Foods Show in Savannah, Georgia, they are soon confronted with an overbearing vendor, Dolly Jean, who insists *she* is the next Paula Deen. Dolly proves she will go to any lengths to steal the coveted blue ribbon award for best recipe at the Fancy Foods Show, even if she has to lie, steal, and cheat her way to the top including sabotaging Amelia and Cassandra's cooking demonstration in front of the panel of judges. When Dolly ends up murdered by her own low country recipe, the ladies know they've got to take action and find the killer or they may find themselves the next target!

Strong women, strong tea and even stronger friendships are steeped in this mystery. Snuggle up with your favorite pot of tea and prepare one of the delectable recipes from this page turner filled with tea infused recipes.. *The Traveling Tea Ladies-Death in the Low Country* will leave you screaming for MORE!

Coming in 2012

The Traveling Tea Ladies
Tea With an At"TEA"tude Cookbook

A unique compilation of tea time and tea infused recipes from the first three books in *The Traveling Tea Ladies* series. Techniques for cooking with tea as an ingredient, food and tea pairings, and proper tea preparation are included.

CPSIA information can be obtained at www.ICGtesting.com
Printed in the USA
LVOW011325070313

323192LV00008B/85/P